OLD MORMON PALMYRA
AND NEW ENGLAND

OLD MORMON
PALMYRA
AND
NEW ENGLAND

HISTORIC PHOTOGRAPHS
AND GUIDE

RICHARD NEITZEL HOLZAPFEL
and
T. JEFFERY COTTLE

F}

1991

Fieldbrook Productions, Inc.

FOR JENI AND MICHAELA

Book design by Richard Firmage
Front cover photograph, Hill Cumorah, Manchester, New York. (One of the many drumlins in Western New York.) Photograph courtesy of California Museum of Photography—James Ricalton, 1904
Back cover photograph, Hauling the Joseph Smith Monument, South Royalton, Vermont. (Construction crew hauling monument.) Photograph courtesy of LDS Historical Dept.—Junius F. Wells, 1905

Library of Congress Catalog Number: 91-071062
ISBN: 1-879786-00-1

Printed in the United States of America

Fieldbrook Productions, Inc.
1901 E. Fourth Street, Suite 150
Santa Ana, California 92705

PREFACE

Photography was not yet invented when Joseph Smith, Jr. (1805–44) lived in New England, New York, and Pennsylvania. The invention of the first viable method of fixing a permanent image to a surface occurred in France and coincided with the establishment of the Latter-day Saints at Nauvoo, Illinois, in 1839. Lucian Foster, a member of the LDS Church from New York, arrived in Nauvoo in 1844 with the apparatus necessary to fix images of the city and Saints.

In 1846, most of the Saints living in Nauvoo began the great exodus west to the Rocky Mountains, leaving their homes, temple, and city in Illinois. Foster, the first photographer of Mormon people and places, did not follow them to Utah but did leave the first visual record of the Saints at Nauvoo. Later, others applied the photographic art to capture, in time, important Mormon historical sites and places of interest.

St. Louis photographer Thomas Easterly made a beautiful close-up Nauvoo Temple daguerreotype that is now preserved in the Missouri State Historical Society at St. Louis. In Cleveland, Ohio, Thomas Sweeny listed a Kirtland Temple photograph among his own works in the early 1860s (this image is lost). The earliest available photograph of the Kirtland Temple was taken by Mr. Faze from Painesville, Ohio, in the 1870s. The Kirtland Temple was the daguerreotype studio of James F. Ryder in the 1840s, though no known Ryder photograph was taken of the temple itself.

Beginning in the 1880s, Mormons from Salt Lake City were among those visiting these sites as pilgrims. They not only visited historic places but also photographed them as well. Three well-known Mormon historians, Andrew Jenson, B. H. Roberts, and Junius F. Wells, contributed to our photographic record. Jenson, Roberts, and Wells were not professional photographers; but they, along with Foster, Easterly, Sweeny, and Faze, preserved a few glimpses of the Mormon past.

In 1904, the first documented photographic tour of Mormon historical sites was commercially produced by the firm of Underwood and Underwood in New York City. Beginning in 1882, Elmer and Ben Underwood set up an office in Ottawa, Kansas, as a headquarters for a house-to-house selling organization of fine stereographic views (two stereoscopic pictures designed to give a three-dimensional effect when viewed through a stereoscope). Soon, branch offices were opened in Baltimore, in New York, and in Liverpool, England. The company was manufacturing 25,000 stereo views per day (more than 7 million a year) and 300,000 stereoscopes annually by 1901.

Underwood and Underwood hired James Ricalton, a retired New Jersey school teacher, to travel throughout the world to produce photographs for their international stereoscope series. In 1904, Ricalton made his way to the Far East from New York. As he journeyed toward the Pacific Ocean, he photographed Mormon historical sites, beginning in New York and finishing in Salt Lake City. Shortly thereafter, Underwood and Underwood produced a set of thirty-six stereo views from Ricalton's work.

The LDS Church historical set was sold throughout the United States and Europe during the following years. These stereoscope images were the first attempts by a professional photographer to document the Mormon movement that began in New York and ended in the Great Basin of Salt Lake City. According to one scholar, the Mormon Church is "the only religious group that may be said to have a pictorial history in stereo."[1]

A few years later, J. B. King, another non-Mormon professional photographer, issued a set of approximately thirty-six views illustrating the history of the Church, beginning in New York. Unfortunately, the quality of these views is poor and the set is seldom found in good condition.

George Edward Anderson's 1907 trip was the next known attempt to document Church historical places by a professional photographer. Anderson's work, unlike that of Ricalton and King, included New England and significantly increased the number of images of Mormon historical sites. Initially, Anderson photographed sites on his own as he traveled to his proselyting mission in England. Upon his arrival in

Chicago, he met with LDS Church leader George Albert Smith and received official Church approval to delay his mission to England so he could continue photographing important sites of Church historical events.

Since G. E. Anderson's celebrated photographic pilgrimage in 1907, numerous professional and amateur photographers have been adding images to an increasingly large photographic collection of Mormon historical sites. Many of these views can be seen in various books and articles, including our previous work, *Old Mormon Nauvoo 1839-1846: Historic Photographs and Guide* (Provo: Grandin Book Company, 1990).

As we completed our study of early photographs of "Old Mormon Nauvoo" in Illinois, we immediately began researching Mormon historic sites in the Northeastern United States (New England, New York, and Pennsylvania). Although the problems encountered in researching early Nauvoo photographs were more challenging than those in this area known as the "cradle of Mormonism," we still had some concerns regarding photograph identification and historical background. We were aware that over the past few decades and in the most recent publications, several photographs have been printed with misleading information in their captions; and we wanted to avoid similar mistakes in our research.

We found the specific identification of several sites and photographs to be challenging; we base our results on our comparison of several important studies by Latter-day Saint (LDS) and Reorganized Latter Day Saint (RLDS) historians. In addition, we used land records, diaries, journals, and census records in an effort to establish the authenticity of these sites and photographs.

In this book, we provide a verbal and pictorial tour of Northeastern United States historic places that have Mormon significance. While we cannot possibly reconstruct the past, these early photographs allow a visual window to the past in a way other documents cannot. The words of the early Saints help restore the life of this period, as do the photographs we have included. In quotations from journals, letters, and diary accounts, whether holographic writings or printed editions, we have oftentimes spelled out abbreviated words and made some corrections in spelling and punctuation to make the material more readable.

Many of the nineteenth- and early twentieth-century photographs in this book are the earliest-known photographs of their respective sites. When early photographs of sites were not available, we used contemporary illustrations and a few recent photographs. We have included three appendix sections that contain information on the use of *town* and *township*, of sites that still stand or have markers, and of photographic sources and collections and a selected bibliography of published material listing the most-important published research of this period of Church history.

Many individuals helped and encouraged us during our research and writing. Without their assistance, this book would not have been possible. We thank Thomas Alexander, Milton V. Backman, Dan Bachman, Suzanne Barnard, Ron Barney, Charlotte Barry, Seward E. Beacon, Dale Berge, Susan Easton Black, Donald Cannon, Lyndon Cook, Paul E. Dahl, Paul Damron, Edward W. Earle, Don Enders, J. Sheldon Fisher, Rell Francis, Steve Gardner, Brant Jones, Jess Kohlert, Mary Ann Lyman, Veneese Nelson, Stewart Park, Bruce Pearson, Larry C. Porter, Margaret Rich, Ron Romig, Dana Roper, Bill Slaughter, Brian Sokolowsky, Steve Sorensen, Calvin Stevens and L. M. Udall. A special thanks to Ted D. Stoddard, who was our primary editor, and to Richard Firmage, who designed the book.

Many institutions have graciously provided copies of photographs and permission for their reproduction. We thank the Avon Historical Society, Boston Public Library, Bostonian, Brigham Young University Harold B. Lee Library Archives, Buffalo and Erie County Historical Society, California Museum of Photography, Columbia University, The Church of Jesus Christ of Latter-day Saints Church Educational System College Curriculum Department, Historical Department, and Visual Resources Library, Dartmouth College Library Special Collections, Essex Institute, Historical Society of Pennsylvania, New York Historical Society, North Haven Historical Society, Old York Historical and Improvement Society, Peabody Museum of Salem, Perrysburg Historical Society, Rhode Island Historical Society, Rochester Public Library, Sheldon Historical Society, South Royalton Historical Society, Topsfield Historical Society, Tunbridge Historical Society, United States Department of Agriculture, National Archives and Records Service, the Utah State Historical Society, and Wells Historical Society. In making these acknowledgments, we nevertheless take full responsibility for the information contained herein.

Like our previous work, this book relates events as the participants themselves experienced them, using their own statements whenever possible. The early Saints, like ourselves, understood Joseph Smith's early religious experiences quite differently than others did at the time and today. Insofar as the miracles, revelations, and visions were a reality to him and the other Mormons, we have treated them as genuine in this book. Non-Mormon readers will surely have questions about the meaning of these incidents, but at least they will have an understanding of how Joseph Smith and other early Mormons perceived their experiences.

LDS Church leader Elder John Carmack recently wrote, "It is natural to want to know the place of important events. Places such as Bethlehem, Sharon, and Mount Vernon take on significance because of events that occurred there."[2] In keeping with this spirit, we have undertaken to present historic photographs of these "important places" in American religious history.

CONTENTS

PREFACE   v

EARLY HISTORY OF JOSEPH SMITH
AND THE CHURCH   3

MASSACHUSETTS   21

VERMONT   39

NEW HAMPSHIRE   71

NEW YORK   83

PENNSYLVANIA   149

CONNECTICUT   165

MAINE   179

RHODE ISLAND   190

EPILOGUE   194

APPENDIX ONE: SITE INFORMATION   196

APPENDIX TWO: PHOTOGRAPHIC SOURCES   198

NOTES   201

SELECTED BIBLIOGRAPHY OF PUBLISHED
   MATERIAL   209

INDEX   223

OLD MORMON PALMYRA
AND NEW ENGLAND

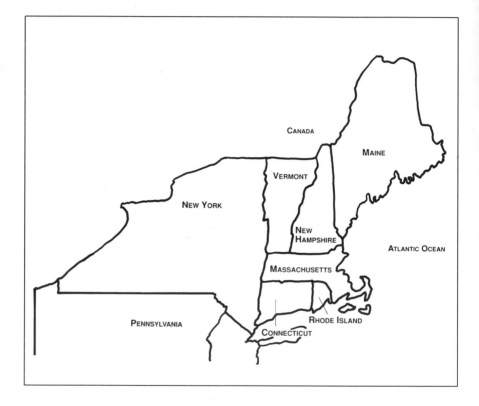

EARLY HISTORY OF JOSEPH SMITH, JR. AND THE LDS CHURCH

George Edward Anderson, a Utah photographer, wrote in his journal on 20 April 1907:

> Bid father and mother goodbye. Bro. Thornburg got grips etc. from depot and Olive assisted me in packing up. Bid all good bye and left Springville [Utah] on No. 6 about 10:15 a.m. Snow in canyon and all the way up ... [O]ff at Price and took next section of No. 6 which left Price about 7:00 p.m. Dinner with Joseph Jones, gave me sack of apples and $2.00.[1]

Anderson boarded the Denver and Rio Grande Western Train No. 6 for a trip that would ultimately take him to England. At forty-six years of age, he was beginning a mission for The Church of Jesus Christ of Latter-day Saints.

Though he was bound for England, Anderson did not arrive there until a year later. His delay was occasioned by his photographic work of Mormon historical sites in New England, New York, Pennsylvania, Ohio, Illinois, and Missouri. At first, this adventure was a personal mission for him as he proceeded on his trip to England; but in Chicago this all changed when he met with LDS Church leader George Albert Smith. Anderson recorded:

> Apostle George A. Smith came into Priesthood meeting. Brother Smith told me to meet him [from] 1:30 to 2:00 p.m. and he would look at views and give me what information he could about Palmyra and Sharon. I made notes of the points he gave [and] I asked him if I should sail on the Rebbell that sails on the 3rd. He said, "No, [I should] keep on with the work."[2]

Anderson carried his heavy view camera and traversed the wooded countryside and grain-ripened fields, often sleeping outdoors with only his camera cloth for covering. Seeking the most appropriate views of the sacred Mormon sites, he recorded, "Would like to get the views I can see in my mind's eye . . . Could not get the effect of light and shade I wished." Later, he regretfully wrote, "Need painter's hand to fix colors to do it justice."[3] Like his photographs, his diaries contain precise historical details about these Church landmarks—details that he learned from local individuals.

A few examples of his work first appeared in the *Boston Sunday Globe* on 10 May 1908. A year later, the LDS Church's Sunday School organization in Salt Lake City published a more complete collection of photographs in *The Birth of Mormonism in Picture, Scenes, and Incidents in Early Church History*, written by John Henry Evans and illustrated with Anderson's photographs.[4] Anderson fulfilled his mission in England as he continued to use his skills for the Church's benefit.

After completing his mission in England, Anderson returned to the United States and continued his photographic work in South Royalton, Vermont. After ending his seven-year mission in 1913, he returned home to Utah. His work was a passion. "I feel impressed," he wrote, "with the necessity of making the views. I can see what a

Memorial Cottage and Joseph Smith Monument, Sharon, Vermont
(Birthplace of Joseph Smith, Jr. in 1805)
Photograph courtesy of LDS Historical Dept. — George E. Anderson, 1907★

★(Final line of caption denotes source, photographer, and date of photograph.)

blessing they would be to our people in arousing an interest in this land (Missouri)."[5]

George Edward Anderson's visit to Church historical sites included a trip to Joseph Smith's ancestral home in Topsfield, Massachusetts. There he saw the site of the Smith home and the monument of Samuel Smith in the town's cemetery. Five generations of the Smith family had lived in Topsfield, including Joseph Smith, Sr. (1771-1840), who was born in Topsfield and eventually moved to Vermont.

Anderson arrived in Sharon, Vermont, on 20 August 1907. There he took numerous images of the sites important to the Smiths. In his journal, he chronicled the work he completed in and around Sharon, the birthplace of Joseph Smith, Jr. He mentions the hearthstone and

Solomon Mack Home Site, South Royalton, Vermont
(Part of 100-acre farm purchased by Mack in 1804)
Photo courtesy of LDS Historical Dept. — George E. Anderson, 1907

chimney of the old home as well as the new cottage and the monument stone that had been placed there in 1905, the centennial of Smith's birth.

He photographed the "old Mack home" (Lucy Mack Smith's father's home), which was located in the "hollow below the cottage, near where the water pipe crosses the hollow."[6] The Smith family lived in and around Sharon for several years. They occupied a farm and home in Tunbridge, a rented home in Randolph, and a home in Royalton. Nothing seems to have escaped Anderson's investigation of Mormon historical sites. Eventually, the Smiths were unable to sustain themselves economically in New England. Therefore, like many others during the period, they went west for a new life in New York.

On 2 January 1908, Anderson visited Fayette, New York. There he photographed the site where the organization of the Church took place. At the farm of Peter Whitmer, he saw an "old tree now standing" at the site of the log cabin where the Church of Christ (the original name of the LDS Church) was founded in 1830.

Peter Whitmer, Sr. Home Site, Fayette, New York
(Church organized here in 1830)
Photograph courtesy of LDS Historical Dept. — George E. Anderson, 1908

At the close of 1830, the Church headquarters were still located at Fayette, with branches in Manchester and Colesville, New York, and with several branches in Ohio. From the beginning, Smith and the Church suffered persecution and intolerance. As a result, the Church headquarters moved from New York to Ohio, then to Missouri, and then to Illinois in an effort to build God's kingdom on earth and to escape persecution.

Joseph Smith's religious quest began during the religious fervor of the early 1800s known as the Second Great Awakening. This period was characterized by the spread of heated evangelism that swept upper-state New York with fierce intensity. In fact, revivals in this area west of the Catskill and Adirondack Mountains were so constant and powerful that historians have labeled this ecclesiastical storm center the "Burned-over District." [7]

Joseph Smith, Jr. was born in a small home on his grandfather's farm in Vermont on 23 December 1805. After several moves, his family left New England and moved to New York, near the Finger Lakes region, in 1816. In 1817 or 1818, his religious concern was awakened by the preponderance of several religious meetings, which he frequented. He was only fourteen when he was visited by God the Father

Smith Farm and Sacred Grove, Manchester, New York
(Joseph Smith, Sr. family moved here in 1818)
Photograph courtesy of LDS Historical Dept. — George E. Anderson, 1907

Sacred Grove, Manchester, New York
(Identified as the site where young Joseph retired to pray in 1820)
Photograph courtesy of LDS Historical Dept.—George E. Anderson, 1907

and Jesus Christ in the spring of 1820. This experience is known as the "First Vision."

Anderson's excellent photographic work was more the result of his religious devotion than of his pride in his photographic ability. As he retraced the footsteps of the teenage boy at the Smith farm, Anderson chose a beautiful, clear, spring day for his visit to the Sacred Grove, site of the First Vision. Somewhere on a hill overlooking the Smith farm, he set up his big-view camera and made an exposure of the grove of trees traditionally identified as the Sacred Grove. The picture shows the grove in the distance with several boys in the grass looking down on the picturesque field of newly mown hay. For his next view, Anderson moved down to a country lane and made a composed picture of the boys, with the trees as a backdrop. One of the youths was shown climbing the fence as the other fished in the stream.

He felt inspired upon entering the Sacred Grove itself. As his daughter recalled, "He told us later that when he saw the sun shining through the trees into a small clearing, he knew this was the right place."[8] The well-known photograph of the Sacred Grove shows the silhouettes of the backlighted trees, with a boy standing in the clearing below. This is one of the most striking and dramatic images of Anderson's entire photographic career.

Sacred Grove, Manchester, New York
(Identified as the site of the First Vision)
Photograph courtesy of LDS Historical Dept. — George E. Anderson, 1907

In the following years, Joseph Smith received a series of visions and angelic visitations. In 1823, an angel directed Joseph to a cache of metal plates containing the writings of some of the ancient inhabitants of the American continent. Joseph received the plates in 1827, translated them, and in March 1830 published the translation as the

From the top of the Hill Cumorah, Manchester, New York
(Joseph Smith discovered the gold plates here in 1823)
Photograph courtesy of LDS Historical Dept. — George E. Anderson, 1907

Martin Harris Farm, Palmyra, New York
(Harris mortgaged a section of this farm to finance the Book of Mormon)
Photograph courtesy of LDS Historical Dept. — George E. Anderson, 1907

Book of Mormon. A major benefactor of the young prophet was Martin Harris, a prosperous farmer in Palmyra. On a Sunday morning in August 1907, Anderson "rose about 6:00 a.m.," worked on his camera, and then

> found Martin Harris' farm, now owned by Mr. Bush and for afterwards of 51 years known as the Moroni Hill Farm. Recently came into possession of Mr. Shaw. [It] is beautifully located running north and south of New York Gumbrall Railroad and about two miles northwest from Palmyra and the State road running to Manchester.[9]

Joseph was instructed not only to publish the translation of the ancient record as new scripture but also to reestablish Christ's true church, which had been lost over time. John the Baptist and three of Jesus' original apostles, Peter, James, and John, visited Joseph and his scribe, Oliver Cowdery, and ordained them to the priesthood of God somewhere near the Smith home on the Susquehanna River. Joseph

Susquehanna River, Harmony, Pennsylvania
(Near where Joseph Smith and Oliver Cowdery were baptized in 1829)
Photograph courtesy of LDS Historical Dept. — George E. Anderson, 1907

had relocated near Harmony, Pennsylvania, because of persecution in New York. With this priesthood authority, Joseph organized the Church of Christ on 6 April 1830 in Fayette, New York.

From the outset, the doctrines of the Church challenged the religious, social, economic, and political values of antebellum America. Though the United States had been a seedbed of religious dissent from the earliest colonial times, Joseph's critics were uneasy about a man who claimed continuing revelation and who introduced additional scripture. Their distaste for his doctrines was mixed with their fear of his growing power as believers flocked to the Church.

Missionary success in the Western Reserve area of northern Ohio brought the Church and its prophet from New York to Kirtland, Ohio, in February 1831. Many residents in and around Kirtland were awaiting the "restoration" of the original church of God, and they believed Mormonism fulfilled their expectations. Establishing two Church headquarters, one in Ohio and the other in Missouri, Joseph sent missionaries throughout North America. Converts were baptized and encouraged to gather with the Saints in Zion (Missouri) or in Kirtland, Ohio.

Missouri was the Mormon Zion, a place of gathering. Anderson visited the designated temple site on 24 April 1907. He records the events leading up to his visit:

> I found President Samuel D. Bennion's address and phone number and concluded to go out to Independence, it was after 10:00 when I reached the mission headquarters at 302 S. Pleasant Street. Pres. Bennion [escorted me] five miles to Sister Leonora McCarthy. [She] fixed me a bed, as all [was] full at the Mission Home . . . [I] was thankful to get out of the noise, bustle, and smoke of Kansas City.[10]

The following day, Anderson wrote, "[I arose] at 5:30 a.m., bathed my feet, prayer with Elder Harris, he then took me on to the temple lot." For Anderson, this was a solemn moment of reflection and contemplation. He wrote, "I selected points that I thought would make good views and show the temple grounds so that a person from the outside could see how it was situated." This attitude seems to have been his constant concern, "so a person from the outside could see how it was situated." Anderson's journal and photographs reflect his feeling for the spirit of the place. "I feel it a privilege," he recorded, "to be in this land which the prophet of the Lord designated as the center stake of Zion, where the great temple of our God should be raised."[11]

While visiting Independence, he made other views, including the LDS Church Mission Home, Examiner Office, Liahona Office, and the RLDS Stone Church. In every location, Anderson was met with the gracious hospitality of other professional photographers. In Missouri he wrote,

> Developed negatives at Mr. Evans Davis Studio, very kind. Negatives all came out good considering the dull day . . . [26 April] At Mr. Davis studio before 6:00 a.m. and developed negatives made last evening, felt very well satisfied with the record made.[12]

A day later, Anderson "made negative of Richmond, [Missouri] from hill northwest of town. Also of the tombstone of one of the Eight Witnesses, Jacob Whitmer in the old cemetery." As he moved from one historical site to the next, Anderson continued to feel that he "should have more time to get views of the important points in Church History."[13]

During the same period when the early Saints attempted to build Zion in Missouri, another Mormon center, Kirtland, Ohio, continued to grow. Anderson arrived in Kirtland on 7 August 1907. While in Kirtland, he made "several views" and found a place where the "temple is reflected in Chagrin River." Nature did not cooperate with his venture on this day, as the "wind disturbed the surface too much to get view in the morning." But he did make a view in the evening, though he felt he did "not get a perfect reflection."[14]

The small community of Kirtland grew steadily as members continued to move into the area. The Saints built their first temple there, dedicating it to God on 27 March 1836. The completion of the Kirtland Temple signaled a great "pentecostal" season for the Saints who had sacrificed so much to build it.

At this time, Kirtland was crowded. In addition to the constant stream of immigrants settling there, hundreds of visitors were gathering for the dedication. Church leaders from Missouri were present, as well as many priesthood leaders from other parts of the United States. Recalling the events that transpired during this period, Orson Pratt said,

> God was there, his angels were there, the Holy Ghost was in the midst of the people, the visions of the Almighty were opened to the minds of the servants of the living God; the veil was taken from the minds of many; they saw the heavens opened; they beheld the angels of God; they heard the voice of the Lord; and they were filled from

Kirtland Temple, Kirtland, Ohio
(Dedicated by the Church in 1836)
Photograph courtesy of LDS Historical Dept. — George E. Anderson, 1907

the crown of their heads to the soles of their feet with the power and inspiration of the Holy Ghost. . . . In that Temple, set apart by the servants of God, and dedicated by a prayer that was written by inspiration, the people were blessed as they never had been blessed for generations and generations.[15]

Within two years, however, contention among the Saints and conflict with their neighbors caused Joseph Smith and other Church members to flee Ohio for safety reasons. Traveling through Indiana and Illinois, they crossed the Mississippi River at Quincy and made their way across the state of Missouri to Far West, an important Mormon community at the time. By midsummer of 1838, most of the Saints had left the Kirtland area, abandoning their homes, businesses, and farms as well as their beautiful temple.

Anderson arrived at Far West, Missouri, on 16 May 1907. He notes that only a few of the original Mormon buildings remained standing. "Just southwest and across the street from Temple Block," he wrote, "is the Re-organized Church [building] dedicated 18th November 1906." Joseph Smith III and Frederick Smith, son and grandson of Joseph Jr., spoke in a meeting attended by Anderson.[16]

Temple Site, Far West, Missouri
(Dedicated by Church leaders in 1839)
Photograph courtesy of LDS Historical Dept. — George E. Anderson, 1907

Anderson's journal indicates his interest in Church history, as he records information about how the community looked during the Mormon period. He notes, "John Whitmer's Hotel [was] just south of the Temple [site], see old barn [and] Joseph Smith's home [was] southwest of Temple [some] 60 rods."[17] The city of Far West as known by Joseph Smith and the early Saints was all but gone in 1907. However, the founding of the original city of Far West in 1838 alarmed the original non-Mormon settlers of the county. The influx of converts into the area was perceived as a threat to the social, religious, and economic stability in northern Missouri, which eventually led the non-Mormons in the area to force the Saints to leave the county.

Anderson arrived at Haun's Mill, a Mormon settlement near Far West, on 22 May 1907. Haun's Mill was the site of the Tuesday, 30 October 1838, massacre of eighteen Mormons by a group of Missouri militia. Anderson made several "beautiful views of Haun's Mill country from [Mr. Blair's and Mr. Chapman's homes on a rise]."[18]

Soon after the Haun's Mill attack, more Saints gathered at Far West. There Joseph Smith and other Church leaders were arrested during negotiations for a peace settlement. Joseph was taken to Richmond and then to Liberty, Missouri, where he was incarcerated for several months. Meanwhile, Apostle Brigham Young took several thousand

Saints back across the Mississippi River to Illinois and Iowa, seeking refuge from the mobs and state militia from northern Missouri. Church leaders, including Joseph Smith, escaped incarceration in Missouri and fled to Illinois.

Like Joseph Smith's exodus more than half a century earlier, Anderson left Missouri and arrived in Quincy, Illinois. He records on 1 May 1907, "at about 4:40 [I] made a view of Quincy while waiting for the train. [The] east side of Mississippi on the bluffs presents [a] striking appearance."[19] Anderson then left Quincy and headed north to Nauvoo, the former city of the Saints. Nauvoo is the place where Joseph Smith centered the Church in 1839.

The Saints' stay in Illinois was short-lived. They built the city of Nauvoo but were forced to abandon it in 1846 after only seven years. The conflict between the Saints and their neighbors became intense in early 1844. This hostility included bolder attacks against the Church and counteractions to quell the dissent, which pushed both the rhetoric and the strategies of the anti-Mormon movement beyond the possibility of peaceful compromise. The anti-Mormon hostility culminated in the murder of Joseph and Hyrum Smith by anti-Mormons at the jail in Carthage, Illinois.

"[I] rose before 6:00 a.m., decided to go to Carthage," Anderson noted in his journal on 3 May 1907. The weather was cloudy and cold that morning. Anderson, the photographer par excellence, always noted weather conditions that would affect his work. When he arrived at Carthage, the county seat of Hancock, Anderson "visited the jail where the Prophet [Joseph Smith] and Patriarch [Hyrum Smith] were killed."[20] A mob attacked the building about 5:00 p.m. while the Smith brothers were incarcerated and killed them. "I saw the hole in the door, made by the bullet," Anderson reflected later in the day when he took time to write in his journal. He took the opportunity to make one view of the jail, "in a snow storm."[21]

The death of Joseph Smith in 1844 received national attention. The *New York Herald* published an extra to announce the death of the Mormon leaders. The editor, writing in a harsh obituary, stated, "The death of the modern mahomet will seal the fate of Mormonism. They cannot get another Joe Smith. The holy city must tumble into ruins, and the 'latter day saints' have indeed come to the latter day."[22]

Although most anti-Mormons believed Joseph's death signaled the end of Mormonism and the end of the city of Nauvoo, they soon learned otherwise as the steady stream of converts continually poured

Water Street, Nauvoo, Illinois
(Nauvoo was established in 1839)
Photograph courtesy of LDS Historical Dept. — George E. Anderson, 1907

into Nauvoo and undertook the accelerated-pace building of homes, shops, and temple. While in Nauvoo, Anderson made "a number of views of old homes" in the city that had been built by the Mormons.[23]

As a result of the continued building in Nauvoo and increases in the Mormon population in Hancock County, the shaky peace that had settled in the county after the Smiths' assassinations ended. The Saints' situation became increasingly unsettled in 1845 and early 1846. Local and state leaders were helpless in their attempts to resolve the conflict. The situation worsened almost to the point of civil war.

During the fall of 1845, Church officials made an agreement with a commission from the state of Illinois that the Mormons would leave peacefully the following spring. The leaders in Nauvoo wanted to avoid further confrontation and a loss of property and bloodshed like they had encountered earlier in Missouri. If property could be disposed of at some price and if enough time were given to prepare, the Saints reasoned that many of the hardships encountered in 1838-39 might be avoided. However, mob activity continued unabated to keep pressure on the Church.

An advance company of Saints left Nauvoo under the leadership of Brigham Young in February 1846, crossing the Mississippi on rafts and flatboats. By September, the majority of the Saints had abandoned the city.

The last struggle between the Mormons still remaining in Nauvoo and their neighbors, known as the "Battle of Nauvoo," ended the Saints' presence in the city. These poor and sick Saints fled to the Iowa shore of the Mississippi, hungry and cold. They camped along the river and waited for help from the prior companies of Saints already on the way west. As these destitute Saints were camped along the river one night, a flock of quail landed in the camp; and the quail supplied the Saints with much-needed food. Anderson photographed the traditional site of the "miracle of the quail," known as Potter's Slough, near Montrose. These Saints settled temporarily at Winter Quarters on the Missouri River.

In the spring of 1847, a vanguard group of pioneers left Nebraska and made their way to the Great Basin where they founded the city of Salt Lake.

Those who did not "go west" organized themselves around alternative leaders, including Joseph Smith III, the eldest son of Joseph Smith, Jr. From the beginning of the LDS Church's inception in 1830, individuals intent on wresting control of the Church emerged among the Saints. In several cases, these dissenters eventually established separate groups made up of fellow protestors.[24]

Potter's Slough near Montrose, Iowa
(Identified as the site of the "miracle of the quail" in 1846)
Photograph courtesy of LDS Historical Dept. — George E. Anderson, 1907

Following Joseph Smith's assassination on 27 June 1844, several factions sought control of Nauvoo's various institutions, including the Church administrative organs. Among the well-known individuals who claimed succession rights to Church leadership were Alpheus Cutler, Sidney Rigdon, James Strang, Lyman Wight, Brigham Young, and Joseph Smith's own brother, William Smith. The movement that eventually became known as the Reorganized Church of Jesus Christ of Latter Day Saints (RLDS) arose in large part out of a schism within William Smith's faction in 1850.

The LDS and RLDS Churches now maintain the majority of Church historical sites in New England, New York, Ohio, Illinois, and Missouri. Many of these sites are open to the public at no charge. The effort to preserve and to restore these sites has taken significant resources, both of time and money. We appreciate the preservation and restoration efforts and hope this book contributes to a better understanding and enjoyment of the history of the Church in New England, New York, and Pennsylvania.

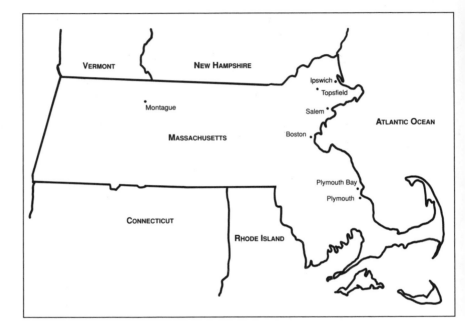

MASSACHUSETTS

The landing at Plymouth Bay on 21 December 1620 was unforeseen by the Mayflower's crew and passengers. Their goal had been the Hudson River lands of the Virginia Company. While they anchored off shore, the religious refugees drew up the Mayflower Compact to serve as a foundation for their new government. They then sailed across Cape Cod Bay and made their landfall.

Those in the Mayflower group were not the first white settlers to arrive in Massachusetts, although they were the first to stay. Only 44 of the original 102 passengers on the ship survived the first deadly winter. Soon thereafter, Salem, Charlestown, and Boston were founded; by 1640, about 2,500 immigrants were living in eight settlements.

The Puritan exodus to North America was motivated by deep religious values and goals. In 1692, the Massachusetts Bay and Plymouth Colonies were combined under the royal governor, Sir William Phipps. Eventually, the theocratic power of the leaders was stripped; and reform moved across New England.

The Indian warfare that punctuated the entire Colonial Period reached a peak in the King Philip's War (1675-76). Eventually, the native Americans allied themselves with the French during the French and Indian War. The New England Colonies not only helped defeat the French forces but also grew independent of Great Britain. The Boston Tea Party, the closing of Boston Harbor, and the organization of the Minutemen all added a spark to the powder keg that lit the explosion of revolution in North America. The Colonials engaged British troops at Lexington and Concord. Life in Massachusetts changed forever as a result of these events. For Robert Smith and his descendants, these changes paved the way for the rise of a New World religion, Mormonism. Robert Smith's great-great-grandson, Joseph Smith, Jr., born in New England, organized the Church of Christ (The Church of Jesus Christ of Latter-day Saints) on 6 April 1830 in New York.

Even before the Church was officially organized, disciples of this new American religious movement had been seeking converts. Such proselyting activity was intensified after April 1830 when missionaries set out with copies of the newly published scripture, the Book of Mormon. By 1831, more than fifty-eight Mormon missionaries proselytized for converts in the United States and Canada. Within another twelve years, more than five hundred missionaries were seeking the faithful in North America and England.

As the word went forth during the first decade of the Church's existence, membership swelled from six persons to 30,000. Massachusetts was one field "white already to harvest." Catherine Spencer moved to Middlefield, Massachusetts, with her husband and family. When Catherine's brother-in-law, Daniel Spencer, visited the family in 1840, her husband, Orson Spencer, was a Baptist minister at the time.

Daniel had accepted baptism into the new Mormon faith earlier and had come to Massachusetts with the expressed intention of converting his minister brother and his sister-in-law. After several days of conversation and lively discussions, Catherine said to her husband, "Orson, you know this is true!"[1] Orson did know; and, as a result, the couple were baptized shortly thereafter. For Catherine, baptism meant family conflict. Her share of her father's estate was revoked. Friends offered her help if she would leave Mormonism. Her reply was, "No, if they will withhold from me the supplies they readily granted to my sisters and brother because I adhere to the Saints, let them. I would rather abide with the Church in poverty, even in the wilderness, without their aid, than go to my unbelieving father's house and have all that he possesses."[2]

After giving up a paid Baptist ministry and a salary that kept them quite comfortable, Catherine and Orson joined the Saints in Nauvoo, Illinois. At the age of thirty-five, a short four years later, Catherine Spencer died in the severe winter weather as the Saints were driven from their Illinois home into the wilderness of Iowa in 1846.

Massachusetts was the ancestral home of several Mormon leaders, including Joseph Smith, Jr. Joseph's mother's family settled in Salisbury in 1669, and his father's family settled in Topsfield. Massachusetts was also the birthplace of a number of notable Mormons, including John C. Bennett, Ezra T. Benson, John F. Boynton, John Corrill, Levi Hancock, Vienna Jaques, Joseph Knight, Sr., Thomas B. Marsh, Isaac Morley, Edward Partridge, Willard Richards, Orrin Porter Rockwell, Joseph Smith, Sr., Eliza R. Snow, Joseph Young, and Emmeline B. Wells. The parents of Brigham Young, Heber C. Kimball, and Willard Richards were born in Hopkinton, a farming community about twenty-five miles southwest of Boston.

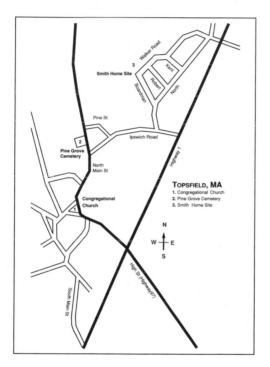

Topsfield, Massachusetts

Topsfield is located about twenty miles north of Boston and approximately twelve miles northwest of Salem.

In 1641, white settlers arrived in the Topsfield area, then known as "New Meadows."[3] Farming was the chief occupation of these people. Religion played a significant role in the lives of the Topsfield inhabitants. By the time the Revolution drew to a close, Topsfield had become

Topsfield, Massachusetts
(Ancestral home of Joseph Smith, Jr.)
Photograph courtesy of the Topsfield Historical Society—Unknown, before 1900

a thriving New England town about twenty miles north of Boston on the north shore of Massachusetts. Five generations of Smiths lived in Topsfield. The Smiths were distinguished by their patriotism, religiosity, and socioeconomic success.

Robert Smith, the first family member, arrived in Massachusetts from England in 1638. His son and grandson, both named Samuel, lived in Topsfield. His great-grandson, Asael Smith, married Mary Duty of Rowley, Massachusetts. To this union was born a son named Joseph Smith (known as Joseph Smith, Sr.) in 1771 at Topsfield. This son was the father of the Prophet Joseph Smith.

Samuel, Asael, and Joseph were baptized into the Congregational Church in Topsfield. Asael and Mary remained in Topsfield until 1791, when they moved to Ipswich and then eventually on to Tunbridge, Vermont.

SAMUEL AND ASAEL SMITH HOME SITE

The Smith home site is located north and slightly east of the Topsfield town center. To get to the home site from the town center, take High Street (Highway 97) to Ipswich Road. Turn east onto Ipswich, and continue until you reach North Street (running north).

Samuel and Asael Smith Home, Topsfield, Massachusetts
(Birthplace of Joseph Smith, Sr. in 1771)
Photograph courtesy of the Topsfield Historical Society—Unknown, before 1875

Turn onto North Street, and continue until you reach Boardman Road. The Smith home site is at the end of Boardman on the west side of the road.

Historical Background

Samuel Smith, Jr. (the great-grandfather of Joseph Smith, Jr.) was born in 1714. He married Priscilla Gould. He moved to New Hampshire in 1772 but later returned to Massachusetts. He served in the state legislature and as the governing selectman and town clerk of Topsfield. He also served as a captain in the militia and on revolutionary committees in Topsfield during the American Revolution.

Samuel Smith's obituary was printed in the local newspaper:

Died—At Topsfield, on Monday the 14th instant, Samuel Smith, Esq., aged 72. So amiable and worthy a character as he evidently appeared, both in public and private, will render the memory of him ever precious. For a number of years he represented the town in the General Court, where he was esteemed a man of integrity and uprightness. His usefulness among those with whom he was more immediately conversant, was eminent. He was a sincere friend to the liberties of his country, and a strenuous advocate for the doctrines of Christianity. "The memory of the just is blessed."[4]

Asael Smith (the grandfather of Joseph Smith, Jr.) was born on 7 March 1744 at Topsfield, Essex County, Massachusetts. He married Mary Duty on 12 February 1767. The Smiths lived in Windham, New Hampshire, sometime between 1772-75. During the Revolutionary War, Asael served as a soldier in a regiment that defended New York's northern border. After the war, the family moved to Derryfield (Manchester), New Hampshire, where they owned a 100-acre farm. Asael served as town clerk from 1779-86. Soon thereafter, he returned to his home in Topsfield until 1791 when he moved briefly to Ipswich, Massachusetts, and then on to Tunbridge, Vermont.

Asael's humor is shown in a poem he wrote to the selectmen of Topsfield when he prepared his tax list:

> To the Selectmen of Topsfield:
> I have two polls, the one is poor,
> I have three cows and want five more,
> I have no horse, but fifteen sheep—
> No more than these this year I keep;
> Steers that's two years old, one pair,
> Two calves I have, all over hair,
> Three heifers two years old I own,
> One heifer calf that's poorly grown.
> My land is acres eighty-two,
> Which search the records, you'll find true.
> And this is all I have in store—
> I'll thank you if you'll tax no more.[5]

Three generations of Smiths lived in the home: Samuel Smith, Jr.; Asael Smith; and Joseph Smith, Sr., who was born there on 12 July 1771.

PINE GROVE CEMETERY

The Pine Grove Cemetery is located just north of the Topsfield town center on High Street (Highway 97).

Historical Background

Several members of the Smith Family are buried in Pine Grove Cemetery, including Samuel (b. 1666) and Rebecca Smith, Samuel Jr. (b. 1714), and Priscilla Smith. Samuel Jr. was a respected member of the community. His obituary, dated 22 November 1785, states, "He

Pine Grove Cemetery, Topsfield, Massachusetts
(Smith Family marker erected in 1873)
Photograph courtesy of LDS Historical Dept. — Unknown, unknown

was a sincere friend to the liberties of his country, and a strenuous advocate for the doctrines of Christianity."[6]

George A. Smith (Joseph Smith's cousin and LDS Church leader), upon his return from a visit to Europe and the Holy Land, helped erect a monument at the Pine Grove Cemetery to the Smith family in 1873. One inscription on this marker reads:

> Samuel Smith. Born Jan. 1714. Died Nov. 14, 1785. Priscilla His Wife. Daughter of Zaccheus Gould. Born Dec. 4, 1707. Died Sept. 25, 1744.

Of this visit, George A. Smith wrote:

> I have traveled to Egypt and the Holy Land, have seen the countries of Europe and met many of their most distinguished people, but I have encountered nothing that gives me more satisfaction than being here, in the graveyard of my ancestors — on the ground where they walked and lived and labored 300 years ago.[7]

Salem, Massachusetts

Salem is located about fourteen miles north of Boston.

The Indians originally called Salem "Naumkeag" or "the fishing place." Roger Conaut, a former Plymouth colonist, led thirty men, women, and children to Salem to begin settlement in 1626. By 1629, the settlers had planted maize and were living in thatch-roofed cottages. These Puritans originally named the village the First Congregational Society of America, but they later renamed the community Salem (from the Hebrew word Shalom), "the place of peace." The settlement was directly tied to the sea in fishing and trading for centuries. Salem was also the site of the famous witchcraft trials in the 1690s.

Derby Wharf, Salem, Massachusetts
(Young Joseph Smith, Jr. stayed here in 1814)
Photograph courtesy of Essex Institute—John S. Lefavor, 1875

In 1836, the Church's financial resources had been depleted as a result of the Kirtland (Ohio) Temple construction. During this period, every effort was sought to obtain capital to offset the financial drain caused by several factors, including Church leaders' increased traveling expenses as they ministered to the rapidly expanding organization. Furthermore, the influx of converts (to Missouri and Ohio) necessitated purchasing and developing property to accommodate the newcomers' needs.

Jonathan Burgess, a Church member from Massachusetts, told Church leaders that "a large amount of money had been secreted in the cellar of a certain house in Salem."[8] The leaders decided to follow the lead in the hopes that if they found the treasure, it would alleviate their financial crisis. Joseph Smith was among those who made the trip to Salem. This trip was the first time he had been in the city since he was a young man. Earlier, his parents had sent him to Salem with his uncle, Jesse Smith, to help Joseph recover from his painful leg operation.

Joseph and Hyrum Smith, Oliver Cowdery, and Sidney Rigdon arrived in Salem on 4 August 1836. In Salem, they rented a home on

Union Street, Salem, Massachusetts
(Joseph Smith lived on this street in 1836)
Photograph courtesy of Essex Institute — Frank Cousin, 1895

East India Marine Society Museum, Salem, Massachusetts
(Church leaders visited here in 1836)
Photograph courtesy of Peabody Museum — Unknown, ca. 1866

Union Street. They spent their time sightseeing, trying to locate the treasure, and preaching the gospel. They visited two buildings that are still standing today — the East India Marine Society Museum, now called the Peabody Museum, and the Lyceum Hall, where Cowdery and Rigdon preached several sermons.

Lyceum Hall, Salem, Massachusetts
(Sidney Rigdon and Oliver Cowdery delivered lectures here in 1836)
Photograph courtesy of Essex Institute — Frank Cousins, 1895

Local newspapers acknowledged their visit and their public appearances. The *Salem Observer* noted,

> MORMONISM. Notices were sent around on Saturday, that Mr. Rigdon, of Ohio, would preach at the Lyceum that afternoon, on the subject of the Christian religion. Having understood that he was a *Mormonite*, we went to the Lyceum, expecting to hear something on the subject of the peculiar doctrines of that sect, and perhaps to get a view of the "Mormon Bible," translated from the Golden Plates said to have been discovered by J. Smith, their prophet! The preacher was a man of very respectable appearance, apparently about 40 years of age, and very fluent in his language.[9]

While Rigdon and Cowdery visited the East India Museum on Sunday, 6 August 1836, Joseph Smith received a revelation (LDS D&C 111) that mentioned their "follies" in paying too much attention to earthly "treasures." Moreover, the revelation emphasized that Salem had "more treasures than one."

Joseph visited the museum on 9 August.[10] Other Church leaders, including Brigham and Joseph Young, met with Joseph Smith in Salem to conduct Church business. After a three-week stay, Joseph, Oliver, and Sidney left Salem and returned to Ohio — without the earthly treasure they originally expected to find.

Several years later, in 1841, Erastus Snow and Benjamin Winchester were sent to locate the other "treasure" mentioned in the 1836 revelation. The *Salem Register* reported, "Mormonism is advancing with a perfect rush in this city."[11] Over one hundred individuals were baptized in Salem, and a branch was organized during this period.

Boston, Massachusetts

Boston is located at approximately the middle of the Massachusetts coastline.

Boston was founded by Puritans in 1630 and named for their former home in England. Boston eventually became the most important and largest British settlement in America. Crowded into the Shawmut Peninsula, the early settlement of Boston was surrounded by water except for a small neck connecting it to the mainland. Violent protest against unpopular British taxes brought military occupation to the town in 1768. Two years later, in 1770, the Boston Massacre occurred when Royal troops fired upon a belligerent crowd, further fueling the anti-crown sentiment in the colony. The Boston Tea Party, the confrontation at Lexington Green on 19 April 1775 on the morning after Paul Revere's famous midnight ride, and the "shot heard 'round the world" unleashed in Lexington and Concord later that day sparked the American Revolution.

While visiting the North Bridge in Concord, Parley P. Pratt wrote his famous missionary tract, "A Dialogue Between Joe Smith and the Devil!"[12] He reported,

> In the spring I went to Boston as a missionary, and on business. I proclaimed the gospel, as usual, while on this journey . . . visiting north Bridge, a short distance from Boston, and having a day's leisure, I wrote a dialogue entitled "Joe Smith and the Devil," which was afterwards published in the *New York Herald*.[13]

Following the Revolutionary War, Boston remained an important economic center. Eventually surpassed in size by New York City and Philadelphia, Boston continued to grow geographically and numerically. The city was renowned as a religious, educational, and cultural center. It was only a matter of time before Mormon missionaries and Church leaders came from the west and arrived in this important city.

Joseph Smith and Newel K. Whitney visited Boston and New York City in October 1832, and they negotiated a loan for almost $20,000 in goods for the Church's new venture of a general store.

LDS missionary Freeman Nickerson arrived in Boston on 30 May 1841 to begin missionary work. According to his journal, his missionary work began in Winchester Hall. During one of his sermons,

> One of the number which was called infidels, began to believe in the truth of the Old and New Testaments, which the world calls Mormonism. The individual was Mr. Abijah Tewkesbury, who opened his shipping office, and seated it, for free preaching. He was the first that was baptized in Boston. Three others were baptized on 8th of January, 1842. I have held fore and afternoon meetings at 82 Commercial street ever since. There was a branch organized in Boston, numbering thirty, including one elder and three priests, on 9th March.[14]

East End, Boston, Massachusetts
(Site of missionary activity in the 1830s and 1840s)
Photograph courtesy of Bostonian Society — Unknown, ca. 1850

Balloon View, Boston, Massachusetts
(Commercial street area, site of an early Church meeting place)
Photograph courtesy of Boston Library — James W. Black, 1860

Tewkesbury had been a partner with a Mr. Cutler in 1836 when their office was located at 80 Commercial Street. In 1842, Tewkesbury established a partnership with Martin Adams and moved offices to 82 Commercial Street (where the Saints first met).[15] Tewkesbury himself lived at 19 Fleet Street. In 1844, he moved offices again, this time to 90 Commercial Street.

Commercial Street, Boston, Massachusetts
(Mormons met here in the 1840s)
Photograph courtesy of the authors—Richard Neitzel Holzapfel, 1990

A year later, Brigham Young and other Church leaders arrived in Boston to hold a Church conference. Young recorded,

> Accompanied by H. C. Kimball, Orson Pratt, George A. Smith, and John E. Page, we crossed the Sound from New York to Providence, Rhode Island; from thence to Boston, where we arrived on the 5th [September 1843], and called on Mr. Tewkesbury, 82 Commercial Street.[16]

From 9 September to 11 September, the conference was held at Boylston Hall, which was located above the market, at the corner of Washington and Boylston Streets. Boylston Market and Hall was built in 1809 at a cost of $39,000 on land valued at $20,560. The old market, built of brick, fifty by one hundred twenty-five feet and three stories high, was opened on 14 November 1809. The first floor consisted of twelve stalls for markets; the second floor consisted of four spacious rooms; and the third floor was a hall fifty by one hundred feet and twenty-four feet high. The hall, equipped with an organ, was

Boylston Market and Hall, Boston, Massachusetts
(Mormon conferences were held here in the 1840s)
Photograph courtesy of Bostonian Society—Unknown, ca. 1870

the home of the Handel and Haydn Society from about 1817. This
hall was used for other meetings, including LDS Church conferences.

Eight members of the Twelve were present at the conference, which
was attended by elders and members from all the New England States.
Brigham Young preached at the conference, which "many of the citizens also attended, some of whom were very rude and unmannerly in
their behavior; it was evident that either their parents had not taught
them good manners, or they had made bad use of their early education."
Young commented, "I never saw more a spirit of rowdyism manifest
in any congregation where I ever preached, than was manifested in the
good, Christian city of Boston."[17]

A convert, who at the time was not LDS, left the following account
of one of his many visits to Boylston Hall to hear Mormon missionaries preach. H. Larkin Southworth recorded,

In the evening went to hear Mr. G. A. Adams, the Mormon. The house was crowded as usual. He told me some new and interesting things. First, that the soul is the body and the spirit. Genesis 2:7, "And the Lord God formed man of the dust of the ground and breathed into his nostrils the breath of life; and man became a living soul." Second, that the serpent was the most subtle beast of the field. He said that he had the powers of speech, but he deferred saying anything more on the subject till some future time. Mr. Adams told a great many things that I never thought of before. All were very interesting to me. [18]

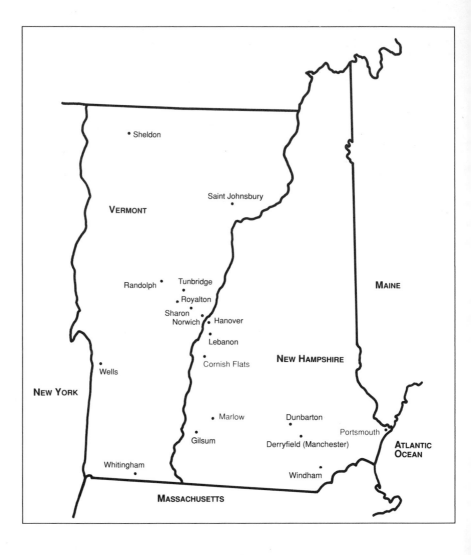

VERMONT

For nearly a century and a half after Samuel de Champlain's initial expedition into the region in 1609, the area around Lake Champlain remained in French control. Several fortifications were erected against the threat of attack by the Iroquois Indians. By the early 1700s, the Iroquois were in league with the French, attacking the British settlements that were being established northward from Massachusetts and Connecticut.

The first permanent English community began in 1724 with the establishment of Fort Dummer near present–day Brattleboro. Eventually, in 1759, the French abandoned their claims to possession of New England lands. Meanwhile, the New Hampshire government had made land grants in Vermont under the assumption that this colony, like Connecticut and Massachusetts, extended to a line west of the Hudson. To the Crown, New York immediately protested the validity of these grants. England backed New York's claims, and New York attempted to settle with those who had land in Vermont by requiring them to repurchase their holdings from Albany. Ethan Allen led a protest in 1770 when he organized local militia units to protect the settlers. This group of militia became known as the Green Mountain Boys.

Many of these "Green Mountain Boys" were involved in the only Revolutionary battle in Vermont, at Hubbardton. Eventually, at the conclusion of these actions, a convention at Westminster declared independent statehood for Vermont under the name of New Connecticut.

New Connecticut soon became Vermont, and for the next fourteen years was an independent republic, coining its own money, running its own postal service, and carrying on diplomatic relations with "foreign" governments. After settling the old land issue with New York State in 1789, Vermont prepared to become the fourteenth state, the first under the new U.S. Constitution in 1791. At this time, Asael Smith arrived in Vermont from Massachusetts.

Asael was a Universalist, who believed in Jesus Christ, a God of love who would save all His children. Asael "always knew that God was going to raise up some branch of his family to be a great benefit to mankind."[1] When his son, Joseph Smith, Sr., presented him a copy of the Book of Mormon, he was very enthusiastic. He died in the fall of 1830, confident that his grandson, Joseph Smith, Jr., was his long-anticipated prophet who had heralded in a new religious age to the world.

Jared Carter may have been the first LDS missionary in Vermont following the organization of the Church in New York. He arrived in Vermont sometime in 1831 and baptized twenty-seven people in Benson, Rutland County. A branch of the Church was organized there during his visit. The following year, in 1832, Orson Pratt and Lyman E. Johnson arrived at Charleston, Vermont, and baptized fourteen converts, including Winslow Farr, William Snow, and Zerrubbabel Snow. Jared and Simeon Carter baptized another large group of people at the end of the year during their missionary trip to Vermont.

Erastus Snow was converted by Orson Pratt during Pratt's visit to Vermont in 1832. As a young man, Snow worked in the mills that had been established in the area and attended the school that his father helped build and support. The first message of the restoration arrived in St. Johnsbury by Levi Snow's son, Zera, during a brief visit home. Soon thereafter, Orson Pratt and Lyman E. Johnson came to St. Johnsbury in 1832. Erastus was eighteen years of age at the time. The first preaching occurred in Snow's barn. Erastus recalled,

> I heard Elder Pratt's message. It seemed to me that it must be true; for from the day he sat at our fireside that evening after his first meeting, while conversing on the scriptures and on the revelations and manifestations to Joseph Smith, the Holy Ghost descended upon me, bearing witness that what he was telling was the truth and that they, these Elders, were messengers from God. I began to read the *Book of Mormon*, and so absorbed was I that I felt cheated to have to eat, work, and sleep. I did as Moroni asked me to do, and through the Holy Ghost I did receive the assurance of its truth.[2]

Pratt's missionary activity in New England began with an appointment by revelation in 1832.[3] Pratt records the following:

> Elder L. E. Johnson and myself started on our eastern mission, traveling, as usual, on foot, without purse or scrip, and carrying our change of clothing in our hands. We traveled in an easterly direction through Ohio, Pennsylvania, New Jersey, New York City, to Hurlgate, on Long Island.[4]

Johnson and Pratt preached some thirty times in villages as they traveled east. In some locations, several people were baptized and ordained to the priesthood. At Hurlgate, Orson baptized his brother, Anson. From there, the missionary companionship traveled north to visit Pratt's parents in Canaan, Columbia County, New York.

Pratt and Johnson left Canaan and visited southern Vermont and New Hampshire and eventually traveled up the Connecticut River to Bath, New Hampshire. Pratt concentrated his missionary labors in this region until he returned to the Church headquarters in Kirtland, Ohio, on 17 February 1833. Pratt wrote,

> having been absent on this eastern mission one year and fourteen days, during which we traveled on foot near 4,000 miles, attended 207 meetings mostly in places where they had not heard the work; baptized 104 persons and organized several new branches of the church.[5]

Many of the early members and leaders of the Church were born in Vermont. Joseph Smith, Jr.'s brothers, Alvin, Hyrum, and Samuel, and his sister, Sophronia, were born in Tunbridge. William and Ephraim were born at Royalton, Don Carlos was born at Norwich, and Joseph himself was born at Sharon, Vermont. Other notable Mormons born in Vermont include Albert Carrington, Warren and Oliver Cowdery, Jacob Gates, Lyman and Luke Johnson, Heber C. Kimball, Zera Pulsipher, Erastus Snow, Newel K. Whitney, and Brigham Young.

Tunbridge, Vermont

Tunbridge is located almost equally between the north and south borders of Vermont and fifteen miles west of the New Hampshire border. Tunbridge is approximately five miles north of South Royalton.

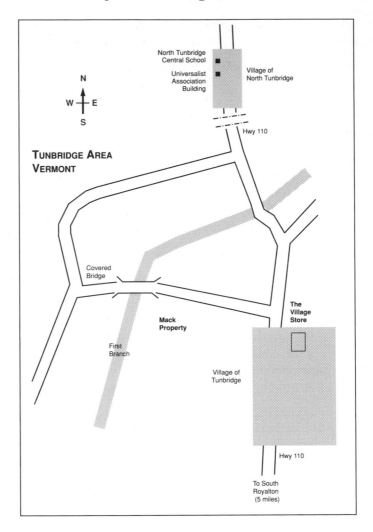

To a council meeting held at Portsmouth, New Hampshire, Governor Benning Wentworth presented a plan that had been made by Joseph Blanchard in 1761. Several new towns were proposed from the northernmost end of Charlestown, New Hampshire, to the northerly end of a place called Coos (Newbury, Vermont). Wentworth named many of the new townships himself, among them Tunbridge. Though the origin of this name is obscure, the town may have been named after William Henry Zulestein de Nassau, the fourth Earl of Rochford, Viscount Tunbridge of Tunbridge.

Tunbridge, Vermont
(The Joseph Smith, Sr. family lived in this vicinity for six years)
Photo courtesy of the Topsfield Historical Society — Unknown, 1890

Settlement of the Tunbridge area was slow. Only a few individuals settled in Tunbridge before the Revolution. A British scouting party
attacked Tunbridge on 16 October 1780 with a force of about three
hundred Indians. They destroyed the harvest, burned many homes,
and killed two men. Eventually, local militia units arrived to find the
British in retreat across the White River. Only three families stayed in
Tunbridge during the winter following the attack. After the conclusion of the Revolutionary War in 1781, immigration to Vermont and
Tunbridge increased.

The town was officially organized following the settlement of
boundary disputes on 21 March 1786. Originally, however, only fifty

families lived within its boundaries. Travel was difficult, and for several years the town lacked a church or a schoolhouse. Eventually, more people moved to the community; and homes, stores, and a church were built. The Smith family frequented a store owned by Lucy Mack Smith's brother. Here Lucy and Joseph Smith, Sr. met and were eventually married in the town hall. The Smiths had three sons born in Tunbridge—Alvin, Hyrum, and Samuel Harrison—and a daughter, Sophronia.

Joseph Smith, Sr.'s father, Asael Smith, wrote a family address in 1799 from his home in Tunbridge. His words reveal his Christian beliefs and idealism. The following is an extract:

> My Dear Selfs, I know not what leisure I shall have at the hour of my death to speak unto you . . . and now my dear children, let me pour out my heart to you and speak first to you of immortality in your souls. Trifle not in this point: the soul is immortal. You have to deal with an infinite majesty . . . trifle not with his name nor with his attributes, nor call him to witness to anything but is absolute truth; nor then, but when sound reason on serious consideration requires it. And as to religion, I would not wish to point out any particular form to you, but first I would wish you to search the scriptures and

North Tunbridge, Vermont
(Joseph Smith, Sr. was involved in the Universalist Association located here)
Photograph courtesy of the Topsfield Historical Society—Unknown, 1906

consult sound reason, and see if they (which I take to be two witnesses that stand by God of the whole earth) are not sufficient to
evince to you that religion is a necessary theme . . . If you find that
you stand in need of a Savior, Christ saith: "Look unto me and be ye
saved all ye ends of the earth." Then look to him . . . To him I com-
mit your souls, bodies, estates, names, characters, lives, deaths and
all—and myself, waiting when he shall change my vile body and
like his own most glorious body.[6]

Joseph and Lucy worked their farm in Tunbridge for six years.
Early in 1802, they rented out their home and farm and moved to
Randolph, a neighboring village about seven miles west. The Smiths
opened a store in Randolph with a line of goods purchased on credit
from Boston. During this period, Joseph Smith, Sr. became involved
in a ginseng root venture. The root, which grew naturally in Vermont, was collected and shipped to China, where it had a high value.
The deal went awry, and Smith lost his entire investment. Consequently, he was unable to pay the store payment due on his line of
credit.

This business venture was a significant turning point in the family's
finances. The loss of money from this venture and the debt in Boston
forced Joseph and Lucy to sell their farm, an event that blighted the
family fortunes for the next thirty years. During the next fourteen
years, they moved many times. Between 1803 and 1811, all these moves
were in the Tunbridge-South Royalton vicinity and probably never
involved a distance of more than five or six miles. During this period,
Joseph rented a farm from Lucy's family. He also taught school during the winter.

The family's circle of moves widened when, in 1811, they moved
to Lebanon, New Hampshire. Shortly thereafter, they returned to Vermont, settling at Norwich for several years; and then, in 1816, they
moved to New York.[7]

Another significant event for Lucy during her stay in Vermont
was her experience with religion. "While we were living in the town
of Tunbridge, my mind became deeply impressed with the subject of
religion," she later said. It "probably was occasioned by my singular
experience during my sickness at Randolph," she explained.[8] She
attended Methodist meetings in an attempt to satisfy her religious
desires, while her husband remained aloof from organized religious
groups. Nevertheless, both Lucy and Joseph Sr. had several religiously-
oriented dreams in Vermont.

Tunbridge Village Store, Tunbridge, Vermont
(Identified as where Joseph and Lucy Mack Smith met in 1795)
Photograph courtesy of Charlotte Barry—Unknown, 1917

VILLAGE STORE

The Village Store is located on the main street (Highway 110) of Tunbridge on the east side just north of the public library and town hall.

Historical Background

Joseph Smith, Sr. met Lucy Mack Smith in Tunbridge at the mercantile store. Lucy, born in Gilsum, New Hampshire, in 1775, was visiting relatives in Tunbridge when she met Joseph Sr. Soon thereafter, on 24 January 1796, Lucy and Joseph were married by Justice of the Peace Seth Austin. Lucy wrote, "While I remained in Tunbridge, I became acquainted with a young man by the name of Joseph Smith, to whom I subsequently married."[9]

Universalist Meeting House, North Tunbridge, Vermont
(Asael, Jesse, and Joseph Sr. were founding members)
Photograph courtesy of the Tunbridge Historical Society — Unknown, before 1920

NORTH TUNBRIDGE UNIVERSALIST MEETING HOUSE

The Universalist Meeting House is located in North Tunbridge approximately two miles north of Tunbridge.

Historical Background

Five Congregationalist clergymen converted to Universalism not far from Tunbridge in 1790. Universalists were believing Christians who held that Christ redeemed all mankind by His atonement. Vermont was a stronghold of Universalism during this period. In 1797, the Tunbridge town clerk recorded a request of seventeen members of the Tunbridge Universalist Association, including Joseph Smith, Sr., to be exempted from ecclesiastical taxes. Joseph Smith, Sr. may have financially and physically contributed to the building's erection. Asael Smith moderated its founding meeting; and his two sons, Joseph and Jesse, were among its members.

Within several years and following significant Congregationalist and Presbyterian missionary activities, Universalism began to wane in

Vermont. Asael Smith's own children gravitated toward orthodoxy and, in 1798, Asael himself occupied a pew in the new Congregational Church. Of Asael's family, only Joseph Smith, Sr. remained aloof from conventional religion and refused to join any church.

JOSEPH SMITH, SR. FARM SITE

The Joseph Smith, Sr. farm site was located approximately three miles north of South Royalton just west of Highway 110. The area was originally known as "Tunbridge Gore." A "gore" was a parcel of land triangular in shape.

Historical Background

Lucy recalled her move to the farm in Tunbridge and her life during this period by saying:

> Soon after I was married I went with my husband to see my parents . . . Having visited my father and mother, we returned again to Tunbridge, where my companion owned a handsome farm, upon which we settled ourselves and began to cultivate the soil. We lived on this place about six years, tilling the earth for a livelihood. In

Tunbridge Gore, Vermont
(Birthplace of Alvin, Hyrum, Sophronia, and Samuel Smith)
Photograph courtesy of Harold B. Lee Library, B.Y.U. — George E. Anderson, 1907

Tunbridge Gore, Vermont
(Joseph Smith, Sr. farm located here)
Photograph courtesy of LDS Historical Dept. — George E. Anderson, 1907

1802, we rented our farm in Tunbridge and moved to the town of
Randolph . . . When we came to this place we had two children,
Alvin and Hyrum.[10]

Randolph, Vermont

Randolph is located approximately eight miles northwest of South
Royalton and is located just west of Interstate 89.

In 1778, several men led by Captain Aaron Storrs formed a company for the purpose of buying a town. They were interested in the
area of Randolph, but the state of New York had already granted the
land to another group who had made no effort to settle the area. Storrs'
group decided to try to buy the Randolph area but were unable to do
so. They then requested a charter from the state of Vermont. Their
charter was granted 29 June 1781 under the name of Randolph. In
1801, the town was granted a post office.

Joseph Smith, Sr. rented his farm in Tunbridge and moved his
family to Randolph in 1802. Stephen Mack, Lucy's brother and a mer-
chant, persuaded Joseph Sr. to open a general store in Randolph, which
was larger than Tunbridge and seven miles west. While in Randolph,
Joseph Smith, Sr. again requested an exemption from the Congregationalist tax as he continued to dissent against the dominant religious

Randolph, Vermont
(Joseph and Lucy Mack Smith ran a general store here in 1802)
Photograph courtesy of LDS Historical Dept. — Unknown, before 1900

institution in New England. The request states, "Randolph July 1st 1802. I do not agree in [the] religious opinions with [the] majority of the inhabitants of this town. Joseph Smith."[11]

At the time, Randolph was the largest community in Orange County and the fourth-largest village in the state. Because of the population growth in the area, the venture seemed ideal. Joseph obtained a line of credit and goods from a supplier in Boston. He also became interested in brokering, in China, an herb called ginseng grown by farmers in Vermont. Unfortunately, he was cheated in the venture and was forced to sell his farm in Tunbridge to cover his venture. The Smiths were financially destitute and sought refuge with their relatives in Tunbridge.

Sharon, Vermont

Sharon is located approximately six miles east and slightly south of South Royalton and is located just south of Interstate 89.

On 17 August 1761, the town of Sharon was chartered. It probably received its name from Sharon, Connecticut, because most of the town's grantees and many of the subsequent settlers were from there. Sharon initially grew quite rapidly and received its first post office in 1811. However, by 1840, its population had begun to decline.

Solomon Mack, Joseph Smith's maternal grandfather, lived in Lyme, Connecticut, until 1761, when he moved to Marlow, New Hamp-

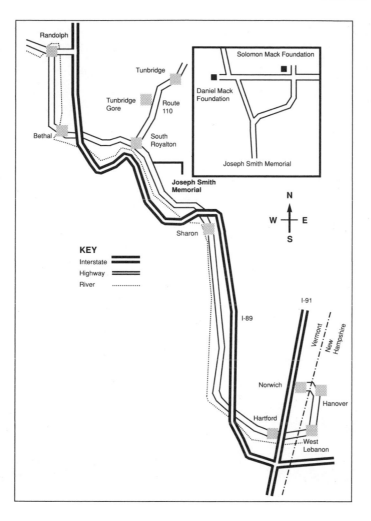

shire. He eventually moved to Tunbridge in 1799 (after a brief stay in Gilsum, New Hampshire, where his daughter, Lucy Mack Smith, was born). Several Macks owned property and built homes near the present location of the Joseph Smith Memorial in Sharon, Vermont. Solomon Mack purchased 100 acres bridging the Sharon–Royalton line on 27 August 1804.

When Joseph and Lucy Smith sold their Tunbridge farm, the sale necessitated their removal to the town of Royalton. They were there only a few months before they decided to rent a piece of farm land from Solomon Mack in Sharon, an adjoining town on the east. While

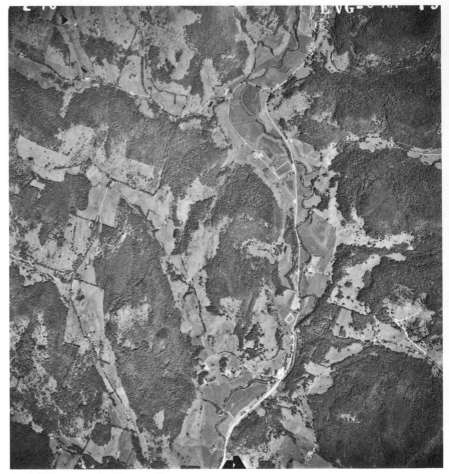

Aerial Photograph, Sharon, Vermont
(Site of Solomon Mack Farm)
Photograph courtesy of USDA–ASCS Aerial Photography — Unknown, 1970

living there, Lucy Mack Smith delivered a son, named after her husband, Joseph. The doctor who delivered Joseph Smith, Jr. is reported
to have been Dr. Joseph Adam Denison. John D. Spring, a Denison's
descendant, recounted a story his aunt told him. She had cleaned out
Dr. Denison's home following his death. She threw out his diary; but
before she did so, she read it. It reported the birth of a son at the Smith
home. Under a later date, he put a note on the same entry saying, "If I
had known how he was going to turn out I'd have smothered the little
cuss."[12]

Panoramic View of Mack Farm, Sharon, Vermont
(Joseph Smith, Sr. rented a farm here in 1805)
Photograph courtesy of LDS Historical Dept. — George E. Anderson, 1907

While at Sharon, Joseph Smith, Sr. cultivated the farm in the summer and taught school in the winter. "In this way," Lucy Mack Smith reported, "our circumstances gradually improved, until we found ourselves quite comfortable again."[13] Joseph and Lucy lived here for approximately three years before their removal to New Hampshire.

SOLOMON MACK FARM

The Solomon Mack farm is located southeast of South Royalton and northeast of Sharon. To get to the farm site from South Royalton, take Highway 14 south paralleling the White River. After traveling on Highway 14 approximately one mile, turn east on Dairy Hill Road and follow it to the farm site (about two miles). The Solomon Mack farm site has two home foundations still visible — the Solomon Mack home site and the Daniel Mack home site. An old stone bridge still may be seen near the Solomon Mack home site.

Historical Background
Solomon Mack was born on 15 September 1732 at Lyme, New

London, Connecticut. He married Lydia Gates on 4 January 1759. A marker at the foundation of the Solomon Mack home site states:

> Solomon Mack Home. The Solomon Mack Farm. 100 acres was purchased by him in 1804. An extra house on it was rented to his son-in-law Joseph Smith, Sr. This old cellar is all that remains of the Solomon Mack home. Nearby may be seen [the] foundation for the out buildings.

The Old Stone Bridge Marker states:

> Old Stone Bridge. This Bridge is typical of the early small bridges in New England. It is made entirely of stone and was here before 1804. When the Solomon Mack Family purchased the farm, the Old Turnpike which was the main highway through this country crossed this bridge at that time.

Solomon Mack Home Site, Sharon, Vermont
(Solomon Mack was the grandfather of Joseph Smith, Jr.)
Photograph courtesy of LDS Historical Dept. — George E. Anderson, 1907

JOSEPH SMITH, SR. HOME SITE

The Joseph Smith, Sr. home site is located on the Solomon Mack Farm adjacent to the LDS Church Visitors Center and Joseph Smith Monument (Memorial).

Historical Background
Joseph Smith, Jr. was born on 23 December 1805 at Sharon, Windsor County, Vermont. He married Emma Hale on 18 January 1827 at South Bainbridge, New York. He was baptized on 15 May 1829. Following his "First Vision" in the spring of 1820 and succeeding visions and revelations, Joseph translated the Book of Mormon and organized the Church of Christ on 6 April 1830. He was sustained as the "First Elder" and eventually as President of the Church.

Lucy Mack Smith wrote the following about this period in Sharon:

> After selling the farm at Tunbridge, we moved only a short distance, to the town of Royalton. Here we resided a few months, then moved again to Sharon, Windsor County, Vermont. In the latter place, my husband rented a farm of my father, which he cultivated in the summer, teaching school in the winter. In this way my husband continued laboring for a few years, during which time our circumstances gradually improved, until we found ourselves quite comfortable again. In the meantime we had a son, whom we call Joseph, after the name of his father; he was born December 23, 1805. I shall speak of him more particularly by and by.[14]

The Joseph Smith, Sr. home was a log cabin built upon a prominence that has been known as "Dairy Hill." The bedroom in which Joseph was born was in Sharon township, while the remainder of the log cabin was in Royalton township.

JOSEPH SMITH, JR. MONUMENT (MEMORIAL)

The Joseph Smith, Jr. Monument (Memorial) is located on the Solomon Mack farm near the LDS Church Visitors Center.

Historical Background
In the spring of 1905, Junius F. Wells, on assignment from the LDS Church's First Presidency, arrived in Sharon, Vermont, to pinpoint the site of the Joseph Smith, Sr. farm and to buy the land for the

Church. Soon thereafter, the property was purchased; and a decision was made to erect a monument on the one hundredth anniversary of the Prophet's birth, 23 December 1905. Two local firms, R. C. Bow-

Joseph Smith Monument, Sharon, Vermont
(Stone setting in 1905)
Photograph courtesy of LDS Historical Dept. —Junius F. Wells, 1905

ers Company and the firm of Marr and Gord, were given the contract to furnish and to erect the monument. The stone was a single shaft that measures thirty-eight and one-half feet long, one foot for each year of Joseph Smith, Jr.'s life.

The inscription on the monument reads:

Sacred to the memory of JOSEPH SMITH THE PROPHET, Born here, 23rd December, 1805. Martyred, Carthage, Illinois, 27th June, 1844.

On the opposite side:

TESTIMONY OF JOSEPH SMITH.

In the Spring of the year of our Lord 1820 The Father and Son appeared to him in a glorious vision, called him by name and instructed him.

Thereafter heavenly angels visited him and revealed the principles of the Gospel, restored the authority of the Holy Priesthood, and the organization of the Church of Jesus Christ in its fullness and perfection.

Memorial Cottage and Joseph Smith Monument, Sharon, Vermont
(Monument dedicated here in 1905)
Photograph courtesy of LDS Historical Dept.—George E. Anderson, 1907

The engraved plates of the Book of Mormon were given him by the angel Moroni. These he translated by the gift and power of God.

He organized The Church of Jesus Christ of Latter-day Saints on the sixth day of April, 1830 with six members.

He devoted his life to the establishment of this Church and sealed his testimony with his blood.

In his ministry he was constantly supported by his brother Hyrum Smith, who suffered martyrdom with him.

Over a million converts to this testimony have been made throughout the world; and this monument has been erected in his honor to commemorate the one hundredth anniversary of his birth, by members of the Church which he organized.

They love and revere him as a prophet of God, and call his name blessed forever and ever, Amen.

Around the capstone above the die:

If any of you lack wisdom, let him ask of God, that giveth to all men liberally, and upbraideth not; and it shall be given him. James 1:5

The dedicatory service was held on 23 December 1905 in a small cottage erected at the site, over the hearthstone of what once had been the Joseph Smith, Sr. home. President Joseph F. Smith (nephew of the Prophet and LDS Church President) attended. In his closing remarks, President Smith said:

Peace be with you, and unto this place, unto this monument, and unto all who come to visit it with feelings of respect in their hearts; and those who come without feeling of respect, may it have the effect of softening their hearts, opening their eyes, and causing them to reflect soberly upon this great problem of human life and redemption that has been opened up to the world through the instrumentality of the Prophet Joseph Smith.[15]

Royalton, Vermont

Royalton/South Royalton are located about 165 miles northwest of Boston. They are located between Randolph and Sharon and just off Interstate 89.

Royalton was chartered in 1769 and was known at various times as Linfield, Lintfield, Loyalton, and finally Royalton. The site was settled in 1771 by Robert Havens of Sharon, who came up the river on

South Royalton, Vermont
(Birthplace of Ephraim and William Smith)
Photograph courtesy of Royalton Historical Society — Unknown, before 1920

the south side. Havens lived in Royalton for five years and then moved to First Branch, a town near the Tunbridge line. An Indian attack in 1780 did not stop other families, most of whom were from Connecticut, from moving into the area. By 1791, one hundred forty-one heads of families lived in town. By 1800, the town had its first thriving village, one that attracted ambitious men and women, including Joseph and Lucy Mack Smith.

After they lost their farm in Tunbridge, the Smiths became tenant farmers and moved whenever the farm was sold or a better opportunity arose. Royalton, like Sharon, was not far from the Smiths' Tunbridge relatives and thus provided some security. While the Smith family was in Royalton, two boys were born. Ephraim was born on 13 March 1810 and died eleven days later, and William was born on 13 March 1811. Joseph Jr. attended school in Royalton at the Dewey Hill School and was taught his letters by Deacon Jonathan Finney. At Royalton, Joseph Smith, Sr. received a vision in about 1811. In the vision, he was traveling in a field covered with dead, fallen timber.

> Not a vestige of life, either animal or vegetable, could be seen; besides, to render the scene still more dreary, the most death-like silence prevailed, no sound of anything animate could be heard in all the field. . . . This field is the world which now lieth inanimate and dumb, in regard to the true religion or plan of salvation.[16]

This vision might explain why Joseph Sr. showed reluctance to join with any organized religion.

School House, Royalton, Vermont
(Identified as the school house Joseph Smith, Jr. attended)
Photograph courtesy of LDS Historical Dept. — George E. Anderson, 1907

Old School House, South Royalton, Vermont
(Identified as the schoolhouse where Joseph Smith, Sr. taught)
Photograph courtesy of Margaret Rich — Unknown, unknown

Norwich, Vermont

Norwich is located on the Vermont and New Hampshire border. The town is on the Connecticut River and is situated opposite Hanover, New Hampshire, approximately fifteen miles southeast of South Royalton.

In 1761, a group of men from Connecticut petitioned Benning Wentworth for four towns in Coos County, New Hampshire. Although they were not granted these towns, they were granted Hartford and Norwich in what later became part of Vermont as well as Hanover and Lebanon located in New Hampshire. In the original charter, the town's name was spelled Norwich; and, until the 1790s, the earliest settlers all came from Connecticut. The town's name came from the grantees' parent town, Norwich, Connecticut; and the first proprietors' meeting was held in Connecticut.

In approximately 1814, Joseph Smith, Sr. moved his family back across the Vermont state line to a rented farm. This was the last Smith home in Vermont—the one they lived in prior to their move to New York in 1816. Their move to New York was precipitated by a natural catastrophe, the volcanic eruption of Mount Tambora in the Dutch East Indies (modern Indonesia) in 1815. The volcanic explosion ejected almost twenty-five cubic miles of debris into the stratosphere, reflecting sunlight back into space and thus reducing the amount of radiation to the surface of the earth.

The dust clouds created by this event reached the northern latitudes in the summer of 1816 and caused adverse effects on the weather in eastern Canada and New England. This climatic change caused widespread crop failures. The summer became known as "eighteen hundred-and-froze-to-death." Many other Vermont farmers, besides Joseph Smith, Sr., decided to leave their rock-bound farm land and move to more promising lands in New York.

JOSEPH SMITH, SR. FARM (SQUIRE MURDOCK FARM)

The Joseph Smith, Sr. Farm (Squire Murdock Farm) is located on Turnpike Road just north of the village of Norwich. To get there, take Route 5 west to Norwich from Hanover to the intersection of Route 5

(Main Street) and Turnpike Road at the red brick building and white church. Proceed left (northwest) onto Turnpike Road and bear left on Turnpike Road until the paved road ends. The house and farm are located on the east side of the road.

Historical Background

Sometime around 1814, the family moved back across the Connecticut River to Norwich, Vermont, from Lebanon, New Hampshire. In Norwich, they rented a farm from "Squire Moredock" and went into business. The stay in Norwich may have been the most economically difficult period of their lives, as they came closer to destitution during this period than in any period before. Several years of crop failure and the fact that the extended family resources were not as readily available to them as in the past, since most of the Smith clan in Tunbridge had uprooted itself and migrated west to New York, brought them to near poverty. Lucy Mack Smith wrote,

> We moved to Norwich, in the state of Vermont. In this place we established ourselves on a farm belonging to one Esquire Moredock [Murdock]. The first year our crops failed; yet, by selling fruit which grew on the place, we succeeded in obtaining bread for the family, and by making considerable exertion, we were enabled to sustain ourselves. The crops the second year were as the year before—a perfect failure. Mr. Smith now determined to plant once more, and if he

Squire Murdock Home, Norwich, Vermont
(Joseph Smith, Sr. probably rented this farm between 1814-1816)
Photograph courtesy of LDS Historical Dept.—George E. Anderson, 1911

should meet with no better success than he had the two preceding years, he would then go to the state of New York, where wheat was raised in abundance. The next year an untimely frost destroyed the crops, and being the third year in succession in which the crops had failed, it almost caused a famine. This was enough; my husband was now altogether decided upon going to New York.[18]

Whitingham, Vermont

Whitingham is located approximately five miles north of the Massachusetts border. The town is equally situated between the east and west borders of Vermont.

The small New England town of Whitingham lies along the Deerfield River, just north of Massachusetts on the eastern side of the southern extension of the Green Mountains. A land rush to this area began in 1797 after a property-rights dispute with the state of New York was settled. The Young family was among these new settlers. John and Abigail (Nabby) Young brought seven children to Whitingham from Hopkinton, Massachusetts. They bought fifty acres of land in Whitingham in November 1800 from a relative. They arrived in January 1801 and established themselves in a vacant cabin. On the first day of June, Nabby gave birth to her ninth child. They named the child after the surname of Nabby's maternal grandparents, Brigham, affectionately called Briggie.

Joseph Young, Brigham's brother, recalled the period shortly after Brigham's birth:

> My father bought a cow . . . The animal would not suffer no one to come near her, except my sister Fanny, who with the infant Brigham in her arms performed this service of milking twice each day during the summer; this was in consequence of the sickness of my mother, and the child had to be nursed from the bottle, and no one could pacify him but my Sister Fanny.[19]

Two markers, one on the summit of a hill in Town Hill Park and the second on the summit of "Brigham Young Hill," or Stimpson Hill, indicate that this area is the birthplace of Brigham Young.[20]

The first marker was erected by the Church and Brigham's descendants. It says,

Whitingham, Vermont
(Birthplace of Brigham Young in 1801)
Photograph courtesy of Utah State Historical Society — Unknown, unknown

Brigham Young church leader-colonizer-statesman. Born in the town of Whitingham, Vermont, June 1, 1801. Leader of Mormon pioneers from Nauvoo, Illinois to the Rocky Mountains arriving in the Valley, July 24, 1847. Became second President of The Church of Jesus Christ of Latter-day Saints serving from December 27, 1847 until his death at Salt Lake City, Utah, August 29, 1877. His statue occupies a place in Statuary Hall, National Capitol, Washington, D.C. This monument erected by descendants of Brigham Young in cooperation with The Church of Jesus Christ of Latter-day Saints.

The second marker, erected sometime before the turn of the century, states, "Brigham Young, Born on this spot 1801, A man of much courage and superb equipment."

After three long and hard years of toil, the Youngs moved again, this time to New York. In the spring of 1804, they arrived in a small community called Sherburne, located at the junction of the Chenango and Susquehanna Rivers.

Brigham later recalled his early childhood in Vermont and New York in these words:

When I was young, I was kept within very strict bounds, and was not allowed to walk more than half-an-hour on Sunday for exercise.

Whitingham, Vermont
(Taken from "Brigham Young Hill")
Photograph courtesy of LDS Historical Dept. — Unknown, unknown

The proper and necessary gambols of youth having been denied me, makes me want active exercise and amusement now. I had not a chance to dance when I was young, and never heard the enchanting tones of the violin, until I was eleven years of age; and then I thought I was on the highway to hell, if I suffered myself to linger and listen to it.[21]

On another occasion, he said,

I never went to school until [I] got into "Mormonism:" that was the first of [my] schooling. [I] never had the opportunity of letters in [my] youth, but we had the privilege of picking up brush, chopping down trees, rolling logs, and working amongst the roots, and of getting [my] shins, feet, and toes bruised . . . I learned to make bread, wash the dishes, milk the cows, and can make butter.[22]

Wells, Vermont

Wells is located approximately fifteen miles southwest of Rutland and thirty-five miles southwest of South Royalton (however, the actual road mileage is much greater).

Wells, Vermont
(Birthplace of Oliver Cowdery in 1806)
Photograph courtesy of Wells Historical Society — Unknown, ca. 1885

Wells was chartered as a town by Governor Wentworth on 15 September 1761. However, the town was not organized until 9 March 1773. In 1780, twenty-three freemen resided in the town. The soil was fertile, and many productive farms were located in the valleys between the mountains. Several important families in Mormon history, the Cowdery (Oliver), Hale (Emma Smith's father), and Lewis (Emma Smith's mother) families, were residents of Wells.

William Cowdery, Jr. located in Wells in 1787. William and his wife, Rebecca Fuller, were the parents of Oliver Cowdery. Oliver attended school at Wells and lived there until his move to Palmyra, New York.

Isaac Hale met Elizabeth Lewis (Emma Hale Smith's parents) in Wells, and the couple were married there before settling in Harmony, Pennsylvania.

WILLIAM COWDERY HOME SITE

The William Cowdery home site is located northeast of the Wells town center. Near the town library is a sign, along with the picture of Oliver Cowdery, that provides specific directions and a map to the Cowdery home site and marker. To get to the home site from the town center, go east on Main Street approximately 0.6 mile and turn north on Saw Mill Hill Road. Follow Saw Mill Hill Road until it forks. Take the fork that veers east (right) and continue a short distance to the marker and foundation on the north side of the road.

William Cowdery Home Site, Wells, Vermont
(Oliver Cowdery marker and father's home foundation)
Photograph courtesy of Stewart Park — Stewart Park, 1990

Historical Background

Oliver Cowdery was born in Wells, Rutland County, Vermont, on 3 October 1806. He attended school in Wells and lived there until he moved to New York. Cowdery married Elizabeth Ann Whitmer on 22 January 1832 in Kaw township, Jackson County, Missouri. Cowdery was one of the three witnesses to the Book of Mormon and later was ordained the "Second Elder" in the Church.

A marker erected next to the remains of the Cowdery home foundation reads as follows:

> Birthplace of Oliver Cowdery. Oliver Cowdery, born here on 3 October 1806, was the principal scribe for the translation of the Book of Mormon and was one of three special witnesses to its divinity. He assisted the Prophet Joseph Smith in organizing The Church of Jesus Christ of Latter-day Saints (Mormons) on 6 April 1830 in Fayette, New York. Over the next few years, Cowdery served in the Church as Assistant President, newspaper editor and historian. He helped compile revelations received by the Prophet and also participated in selecting the restored Church's first quorum of Apostles. Estranged from the Church in 1838, Cowdery rejoined the Latter-day Saints a decade later. He died in Richmond, Missouri, on 3 March 1850, in full fellowship in the faith he had helped to establish.

Isaac Hale Home, Wells, Vermont
(Emma Hale's father's home)
Photograph courtesy of Stewart Park — Unknown, before 1902

Nathaniel Lewis Home, Wells, Vermont
(Emma Hale's maternal grandparents' home)
Photograph courtesy of Stewart Park — Unknown, unknown

ISAAC HALE HOME SITE

The Isaac Hale home site is located approximately 1.8 miles from Wells town center when you are traveling north on Highway 30. The home site is located just east of the highway. This home site was originally the residence of Arah Ward, Isaac Hale's grandfather.

NATHANIEL LEWIS HOME SITE

The Nathaniel Lewis home site was located approximately three hundred yards north of the Issac Hale home site.

Sheldon, Vermont

Sheldon is located in the northwestern part of the state and is situated approximately ten miles from the Canadian border and fifteen miles from the Vermont and New York border.

Sheldon, Vermont
(Birthplace of Heber C. Kimball in 1801)
Photograph courtesy of the Sheldon Historical Society — Unknown, before 1920

In 1790, Sheldon was chartered under the name "Hungerford" because the grant was given to Samuel Hungerford and his associates. Samuel B. Sheldon bought the majority of this land and changed the name to "Sheldon" on 8 November 1792. Apparently, the name is from the Cornish British name meaning a spring, small valley, or the spring in the valley. In 1792, Samuel Sheldon built a sawmill; and in 1797 he built a grist mill. A post office was established shortly thereafter. About this time, Heber C. Kimball, an LDS Church leader, was born in Sheldon.

Presently, a marker in the city commemorates his birth. The marker is located in the Sheldon Creek Cemetery and reads as follows:

> Heber Chase Kimball Mormon Missionary, Apostle, Pioneer and Colonizer. Born June 14, 1801 one mile North of Sheldon Village on the Missisquoi River. Died June 22, 1869 in Salt Lake City, Utah.

Historical Background

Heber C. Kimball was born on 14 June 1801 at Sheldon, Franklin County, Vermont. He married Vilate Murray on 7 November 1822 near Mendon, New York. He was ordained as an original member of the Twelve Apostles on 14 February 1835.

Solomon and Anna Kimball and Heber's parents, following Heber's grandparents and five uncles, moved to Sheldon about the same time. Solomon and Anna purchased two hundred acres just north of Sheldon village near the confluence of the Missisquoi River and Black Creek on 1 April 1799. Solomon participated in community life as a captain in the local militia, a grand juror, and a hayward in charge of fences.

On 14 June 1801, Solomon and Anna's fourth child, Heber Chase Kimball, was born. Heber lived in Vermont for the next ten years before moving to New York during the winter of 1811.

NEW HAMPSHIRE *

The English explored the New England coast for almost two decades before establishing several permanent settlements at Rye, New Hampshire, in 1623. Soon, other communities were established at Dover, Exeter, and Strawberry Banke (Portsmouth). Border disputes and other problems slowed settlement in New Hampshire during the pre-Revolutionary period. New Hampshire, a name given to the area between the Merrimack and Piscataqua Rivers by John Mason in 1629, was the site of bitter disputes among the Anglicans, Antinomians, and Puritan religious communities. Sometime in 1722, several white families located themselves on the Merrimack River near former Penacook Indian settlements.

Asael and Mary Duty Smith moved their family to Windham, New Hampshire, sometime in May 1772. Two years later, the Smith family moved to Dunbarton, New Hampshire; and then, in 1778, Asael and Mary moved to Derryfield (Manchester), New Hampshire. John Smith, Asael's son and later LDS Church Patriarch, was born on 16 July 1781 in Derryfield.

Solomon Mack, Lucy Mack Smith's father, sold his holdings in Lyme, Connecticut, between 1762 and 1766. In the meantime, Solomon moved his family to southern New Hampshire. Marlow, New Hampshire, was the home of several Mack relatives. A decade later, Solomon moved to nearby Gilsum. The Mack family owned a sawmill and grist mill in Gilsum. Solomon and his brother are traditionally identified as the builders of the first bridge and mills in the town. Two children, Solomon Jr. and Lucy, were added to the family in Gilsum.

---

*See map, page 38

71

Solomon and Elisha Mack Mills Site, Gilsum, New Hampshire
(Maternal grandparents of Joseph Smith, Jr.)
Photograph from *History of the Town of Sunderland*—Silvanus Hayward, ca. 1881

Shortly after Solomon Mack moved to Marlow, the Asael Smith family moved to Windham, New Hampshire. Smith moved again to Dunbarton, on the Merrimack River. Following a short stay here and at Salem, New Hampshire, Asael purchased a 100-acre farm at Derryfield (Manchester) on 27 May 1778. His son John Smith wrote, "I was born July 16, 1781 in Derryfield . . . where my father then resided . . . he had held the office of town clerk for many years."[1] Asael moved back to the ancestral home at Topsfield sometime in the Spring of 1786.

Just two years after the LDS Church was organized in New York, the first Mormon missionaries arrived in New Hampshire. In January 1832, Orson Hyde, Samuel H. Smith, Lyman Johnson, and Orson Pratt were commanded to preach the gospel in the "eastern counties." Elders Orson Hyde and Samuel H. Smith left Kirtland, Ohio, without purse or scrip on 1 February 1832 and traveled in Ohio, Pennsylvania, Vermont, Massachusetts, Rhode Island, New Hampshire, and Maine. They baptized many and organized one branch of the Church in Maine, two in Massachusetts, and one in Pennsylvania. Elders Hyde and Smith did not labor alone. They were joined in the eastern states by Hyrum and William Smith, Newel K. Whitney, Lyman Johnson, Orson Pratt,

Stone Bridge, Marlow, New Hampshire
(Solomon Mack built the first wooden bridge at this site)
Photo courtesy of LDS Visual Resources Library—Longin Lonczyna, Jr., ca. 1978

and Simeon and Jared Carter. By the end of 1832, Lyman E. Johnson and Orson Pratt reported baptizing nearly one hundred individuals.

Orson Pratt and Lyman E. Johnson are reported to have been the first missionaries in New Hampshire. They arrived in 1832 and spent 26 days laboring there. Among the 15 individuals they baptized, Hazen Aldrich and Amasa M. Lyman would later play significant roles in the Church. Later that year, Orson Hyde and Samuel H. Smith arrived in New Hampshire. They arrived in the fall of 1832. Hyde mentions his visit to Portsmouth as follows:

> Went on three miles to Portsmouth, New Hampshire and called on W. Foster a printer, to whom we had been referred, but he was gone from town and we come back from the city three miles where we stopped before and left an appointment and tarried all night, but the man became unbelieving and not so anxious to have a meeting because of it. 18th Labored diligently from house to house this day and had considerable energy, but could not get much faith for the people exhorted them to repentance and faith.[2]

Besides Lucy Mack Smith and John Smith, other New Hampshire natives became prominent in the LDS Church. They include King

Follett, John Johnson, William Huntington, Sarah S. Leavitt, Amasa Lyman, Daniel S. Miles, Artemis Millet, Katherine Smith Salisbury, and Mary B. Smith.

Lebanon, New Hampshire

Lebanon is located on the New Hampshire and Vermont border. The town is approximately five miles south of Norwich, Vermont, and Hanover, New Hampshire.

In 1761, Lebanon was established as a town. It was probably named for Lebanon, Connecticut, which was the first pastorate of Eleazar Wheelock, who founded Dartmouth College. Lebanon, New Hampshire, was the original home of the Indian Charity School, which was the forerunner of Dartmouth. Lebanon was actually considered for the permanent home of Dartmouth, but Hanover was selected.

After they left Vermont in 1811, the Smith family lived in West Lebanon, New Hampshire, for several years. Hyrum, age eleven,

Lebanon, New Hampshire
(Joseph Smith, Sr. family lived here between 1811-1813)
Photograph courtesy of LDS Historical Dept. — Unknown, before 1910

attended the Moor's Charity School, which was associated with Dartmouth College in nearby Hanover, New Hampshire.

Alvin, the oldest Smith child, and his sister, Sophronia, age eight, attended public school in Lebanon. The area was known as Poverty Lane. The younger children, Joseph, Samuel, and William, remained at home. Another daughter, Catherine, was born in Lebanon.

JOSEPH SMITH, SR. HOME SITE

The Joseph Smith, Sr. home site is located in West Lebanon on Highway 12A just a few hundred yards south off Interstate 89. The home site was located where the Twin States Cable T.V. Company office is presently situated.

Historical Background
While they lived in New Hampshire, a baby girl named Catherine was added to the Smith family. "We doubled our diligence," Lucy Mack Smith recalled, "in order to obtain more of this world's goods, with the view of assisting our children when they should need it; and

Joseph Smith, Sr. Home, West Lebanon, New Hampshire
(Joseph Smith, Jr. had his leg operation here in 1813)
Photograph courtesy of Margaret Rich—Russell R. Rich, 1967

Poverty School, West Lebanon, New Hampshire
(Where Alvin and Sophronia attended school)
Photograph courtesy of Margaret Rich—Unknown, before 1920

is quite natural, we look forward to the decline of life, and were providing for its wants."[3]

The threat of destitution loomed over Joseph's and Lucy's lives during this difficult period. One more economic failure or natural calamity could put them into perpetual poverty. Another setback now awaited them; this time it came in the form of a contagious disease.

In 1812, over 6,000 people died as a result of typhoid fever in the Connecticut Valley. Every member of the Smith family fell ill with the disease. Young Joseph's fever broke after two weeks, but infection settled in his leg. After several incisions were made between his ankle and knee, a group of doctors who visited the Smith home determined that the infection had entered the bone; and amputation was recommended. Lucy Mack Smith recalled the conversation as follows:

> This was like a thunderbolt to me. I appealed to the principal surgeon, saying, "Doctor Stone, can you not make another trial? Can you not, by cutting around the bone, take out the diseased part, and perhaps that which is sound will heal over, and by this means you will save his leg? You will not, you must not, take off his leg, until you try once more. I will not consent to let you enter his room until you make me this promise."[4]

In the manuscript history of Joseph Smith, dictated in 1838, Joseph states:

> When I was five years old or thereabouts I was attacked with the Typhus Fever, and at one time, during my sickness, my father despaired of my life. The doctors broke the fever, after which it settled under my shoulder, and Dr. Parker called it a sprained shoulder and anointed it with bone ointment, and freely applied the hot shovel, when it proved to be swelling under the arm which was opened, and discharged freely, after which the disease removed and descended into my left leg and ankle and terminated in a fever sore of the worst kind, and I endured the most acute suffering for a long time under the care of Drs. Smith, Stone, and Perkins, of Hanover. At one time eleven Doctors came from Dartmouth Medical College, at Hanover, New Hampshire, for the purpose of amputation, but, young as I was, I utterly refused to give my assent to the operation, but consented to their trying an experiment by removing a large portion of the bone from my left leg, which they did, and fourteen additional pieces of bone afterwards worked out before my leg healed, during which time I was reduced so very low that my mother could carry me with ease.[5]

The operation was performed under the direction of Nathan Smith, professor and founder of Dartmouth Medical School, with no anesthesia for the conscious young boy, who was restrained only by his father during the entire ordeal. The successful completion of the "experimental operation" allowed Joseph to retain his leg, though he walked with a limp the rest of his life.

Hanover, New Hampshire

Hanover is located on the New Hampshire and Vermont border and is situated approximately two or three miles north of Lebanon.

On 4 July 1761, Hanover was granted a charter by Governor Wentworth. However, the first settlers did not arrive until May 1765. The grant was seven miles by seven miles, and the Governor kept a five-hundred-acre tract for himself. This tract eventually became the site of Dartmouth College, the ninth-oldest university in the nation. Dartmouth was founded in 1769 by Reverend Eleazar Wheelock for the purpose of offering a Christian education to native American Indi-

Hanover, New Hampshire
(Site of Dartmouth College and Moor's Charity School)
Photograph courtesy of LDS Historical Dept. — Unknown, before 1878

ans. The first building was a log cabin built by Wheelock in 1770. The campus soon grew to include many colonial brick buildings, the oldest of which dates from 1784.

DARTMOUTH COLLEGE

Dartmouth College is located immediately east of the Hanover town center. Many of the buildings are from the period when the Smith family lived in the area. Moor's Charity School once stood at Main and Wentworth Streets across (west) from the green near Dartmouth Row.

Historical Background

Nathan Smith, the founder of Dartmouth Medical School, was one of the finest physicians, surgeons, and medical professors in the United States. Later, he was also involved in the beginnings of two distinguished medical schools, Bowdoin and Yale. He was an accomplished writer, and his works include a *Practical Essay on Typhous Fever* (1824) and "Observations on the Pathology and Treatment of Necrosis," published in the *Philadelphia Monthly Journal of Medicine and Surgery* in 1827. Both works were important contributions to the treatment of these disorders.

On 23 August 1796, Nathan Smith proposed to the Dartmouth Board of Trustees that a medical school should be founded for the young men of New England who could not attend medical schools in New York or Philadelphia. In 1797, Smith began giving medical lectures at the school. The trustees accepted Smith's proposal, and the fourth medical school in the United States was established. He taught all classes until a former student of his, Cyprus Perkins, was appointed by the New Hampshire Legislature to replace him in 1810.

Dartmouth College, Hanover, New Hampshire
(Nathan Smith established a Medical School here in 1797)
Photograph courtesy of Dartmouth College Library — Unknown, ca. 1870

Most of Smith's work consisted of traveling in a fifty-mile radius from Dartmouth on visits to patients. His students often traveled with him, which afforded them the opportunity to gain valuable experience, as this rural area had no hospital. Ezekiel D. Cushing wrote a letter to his father describing his school days at Dartmouth:

> I am tired to death and have seen more real service since I have been there than ever I did before. In attending the lectures I find more than sufficient to employ my whole time. I have been employed in the lecture room with five others in performing chemical experiments till three o'clock in the morning two thirds of the time since the lectures have begun . . . Last Monday afternoon the Dr. was sent for a man that had a burst in which the intestines had broke through the muscles of the belly . . . Nineteen students with the Dr. at their head set out from Hanover about four o'clock in the afternoon, we stopped twice and arrived at Barre about twelve. We started from Barre at one and arrived at Hanover just at three, all the way on horseback, next day we had two lectures, I went to bed early Wednesday night, but all hands were called up at ten to go to see a boy that

Moor's Charity School, Hanover, New Hampshire
(Where Hyrum Smith attended school)
Photograph courtesy of Dartmouth College Library — Unknown, unknown

had broke his leg twelve miles off. I got home about 3 o'clock in the
morning. Friday noon all hands were called to go with the Dr. to a
boy that had fallen off his horse upon his head. The Dr. thought best
to treat him.[6]

Smith was recognized by Yale University as an able medical professor and organizer. The Yale trustees subsequently offered him the
first position as professor of surgery and medicine at the newly organized medical school, which he accepted in 1813.

Nathan Smith's transfer to Yale from Dartmouth was delayed by
the great typhoid epidemic that spread through the entire Connecticut
River Valley in the winter and spring of 1813. This same epidemic of
typhoid fever struck the Smith family, who lived only a few miles
from Hanover. Following the end of the typhoid epidemic, Nathan
Smith moved to New Haven, Connecticut, and accepted his appointment at Yale University in the fall of 1813.

Dartmouth College was also the site of Moor's Charity School,
which Hyrum Smith attended. Lucy Mack Smith wrote,

Nathan Smith Home, Cornish, New Hampshire
(The principal surgeon of young Joseph's leg operation)
Photograph courtesy of Jeffrey Nintzel—Jeffrey Nintzel, 1988

We moved, as before mentioned, to the town of Lebanon, New Hampshire. Here we settled ourselves down, and began to contemplate, with joy and satisfaction, the prosperity which had attended our recent exertions; and we doubled our diligence, in order to obtain more of this world's goods with the view of assisting our children, when they should need it; and, as is quite natural, we looked forward to the decline of life, and were providing for its wants, as well as striving to procure those things which contribute much to the comfort of old age. As our children had, in a great measure, been debarred from the privilege of schools, we began to make every arrangement to attend to this important duty. We established our second son Hyrum in an academy at Hanover; and the rest, that were sufficient age, we were sending to a common school that was quite convenient.[7]

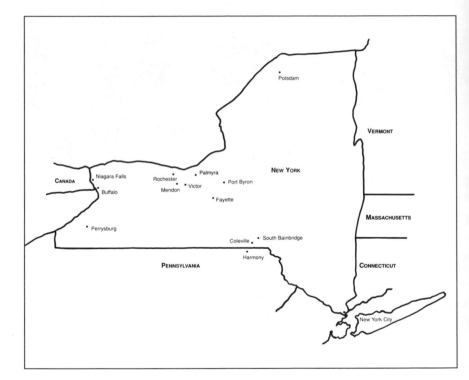

NEW YORK

Originally part of New Netherlands, New York had been an important part of the Dutch West India Company's trading venture. The Dutch supplied the powerful Iroquois confederation of the Mohawk Valley with guns, which allowed the Iroquois to regain superiority over their traditional Algonquin-Huron enemies, who had been armed by the French.

New England merchants watched the growth of trade in the Hudson Valley with envy. Beginning sometime in 1646, a few New England businessmen established a small trucking house on the Naugatuck River near its junction with the Housatonic, about sixty miles from Ft. Orange, a Dutch trading post. Peter Stuyvesant, the Dutch governor, rushed to New Haven and established a treaty between the two nations, which ended Connecticut's efforts to expand. Similar attempts by other colonies eventually forced the issue of annexation by England.

In 1664, Charles II ordered the seizure of the Dutch possessions in America. New Netherlands then became New York, a proprietary province under the control of the Duke of York, who granted its southern portion to other court favorites as the colony of New Jersey.

Settlement in New York did not occur as quickly as might have been expected after English annexation. Powerful trading interests, centered at Albany, blocked the only path that settlers could follow toward the interior—up the Hudson between the towering peaks of the Catskills and Berkshires and westward along the level Mohawk Valley. Schenectady was settled in 1661 by a few families who agreed not to engage in trade with the Iroquois; however, this was the only settlement allowed for some time. Trading interests, along with deficiencies in New York land and transportation systems, slowed the process of settlement into the eighteenth century.

Eventually, settlers from the eastern part of the state and from New England drifted into the war-torn region after 1783. They laid out a few towns that were scattered along the upper Mohawk and Unadilla Rivers, but mass migration did not begin until the Indians were removed and ownership of the area, which was claimed by both Massachusetts and New York, was finally settled. Removing the Indians proved easy, for the ravages of the Revolution and an Indian exodus to Canada left only about 6,000 American Indians in the area. The ownership of the land was settled; and on 1 April 1788, a large area of western New York was sold to Oliver Phelps and Nathaniel Gorham, two land speculators.

While Gorham attempted to obtain financing for the project, Phelps supervised the survey and sales of land, establishing his offices at the foot of Canandaigua Lake. Within a year, over a thousand settlers were scattered over the rolling-hill country of the Phelps-Gorham Purchase. Canandaigua became a bustling town of thirty log cabins, and soon a rival village called Geneva was established at the foot of Lake Seneca. The majority of settlers were from New England. They came west in hopes of finding better farm land and new opportunities.

Sometime in 1816, Joseph Smith, Sr., like many other New Englanders, went west in search of a new beginning. He arrived in Palmyra Village, New York, a few weeks after his departure from Vermont. He left his family behind in Vermont to settle accounts and to prepare for their journey west to a new home.

By 1818, he accumulated enough money for the down payment on a hundred-acre woodland area nearby in the Farmington township. During his first year, he and his sons cleared thirty acres of heavy timber, prepared the ground for cultivation, and planted wheat. By 1821, Joseph Sr. was a father of eleven. He worked hard for his living. In 1822, Farmington township was divided; and the Smith farm became part of the newly created township of Manchester.

Mrs. Palmer, an early resident of the Palmyra-Manchester area in New York, remembered,

> My father owned a farm near that of the Smith family, in New York.
> My parents were friends of the Smith family, which was one of the
> best in that locality — honest, religious and industrious, but poor. The

father of the family was above the average in intelligence . . . Mrs.
Smith was called "Mother Smith" by many. Children loved to go to
her home. My father loved young Joseph Smith and often hired him
to work with his boys. I was about six years old when he first came
to our home. I remember going into the field on an afternoon to play
in the corn rows while my brothers worked. When evening came, I
was too tired to walk home and cried because my brothers refused to
carry me. Joseph lifted me to his shoulder, and with his arm thrown
across my feet to steady me, and my arm about his neck, he carried
me to our home.[1]

The educational opportunities of the children in the Smith family
were limited during these first years in New York because of the rig-
ors of life. The entire family was religious; but only Lucy, two sons,
and a daughter belonged to a church, while the rest remained aloof
from any organized religious group.

During the period of 1817-21, religious revivals were common-
place in this area, which is now known as the "burned-over district."
Several denominations increased in membership; and several churches
built new meeting houses, including the Quakers. Scores of people
were converted to "religion" during this revival period. Young Joseph
Smith, Jr. had his first vision sometime in the early spring of 1820. In
1823, the Angel Moroni appeared to Joseph and told him of an ancient
record. The Smith family was very supportive of young Joseph. His
oldest brother, Alvin, challenged Joseph shortly before his own death,
"I want you to be a good boy, and do everything that lies in your
power to obtain the record. Be faithful in receiving instruction, and in
keeping every commandment that is given you."[2]

In 1827, Joseph obtained the record from the Hill Cumorah, but
local persecution prevented him from working on the translation. With
the help of a local farmer, Martin Harris, Joseph and Emma travelled
to Harmony, Pennsylvania to complete the translation unhindered.
Before he assisted Joseph any further, Martin Harris wanted some assur-
ance that the work was inspired. As a result, Martin took a trip to
New York City to visit Charles Anthon and Samuel Mitchell to verify
the authenticity of the translation. Anthon was at the time professor
of classical studies at Columbia College, and Mitchell was vice president of Rutgers Medical College in New York City. Harris took with
him a transcript of characters from the Book of Mormon.

Harris visited Mitchell, who apparently sent him on to Anthon.
Harris showed Anthon both Joseph Smith's translation and the un-

translated portion of characters from the Book of Mormon. Joseph Smith's history states,

> Sometime in this month of February, the aforementioned Mr. Martin Harris came to our place, got the characters which I had drawn off the plates, and started with them to the city of New York.[3]

Harris wrote:

> I went to the city of New York, and presented the characters which had been translated, with the translation thereof, to Professor Charles Anthon, a gentleman celebrated for his literary attainments. Professor Anthon stated that the translation was correct, more so than any he had before seen translated from the Egyptian. I then showed him those which were not yet translated, and he said that they were Egyptian, Chaldaic, Assyriac, and Arabic; and he said they were true characters. He gave me a certificate, certifying to the people of Palmyra that they were true characters, and that the translation of such of them as he had seen translated was also correct.[4]

Upon his return, Harris threw himself into the work of translation more convinced than ever that Joseph Smith had the gift to translate the ancient record. He acted as scribe for the first 116 pages from

Hill Cumorah, Manchester, New York
(Joseph Smith visited here beginning in 1823)
Photograph courtesy of LDS Historical Dept. — George E. Anderson, 1907

the Book of Lehi. Harris eventually lost these pages in Palmyra. Smith was despondent over the loss of the manuscript. However, he met Oliver Cowdery, who assisted him with the translation until it was completed in the home of Peter Whitmer at Fayette, New York.

Joseph Smith contracted with a local Palmyra book publisher, E. B. Grandin, to print the Book of Mormon. However, Grandin backed down because of local community pressure and a threatened boycott. After some negotiation, Grandin finally agreed to publish the work after Martin Harris offered to obligate himself financially if the book did not sell.

John H. Gilbert, Jr., who was the typesetter and pressman for the Book of Mormon, wrote the following statement in Palmyra in 1892:

> In the forepart of June 1829, Mr. E. B. Grandin, the printer of the "Wayne Sentinel," came to me and said he wanted I should assist him in estimating the cost of printing 5000 copies of a book that Martin

Columbia College, New York City, New York
(Martin Harris visited Professor Anthon here in 1828)
Photograph courtesy of Columbia University—Nathaniel F. Moore, ca. 1845

Harris wanted to get printed . . . A few pages of the manuscript were submitted as a specimen of the whole, and it was said there would be about 500 pages. The size of the page was agreed upon, and an estimate . . . that a page of manuscript would make more than a page of printed matter, which proved to be correct. The contract was to print and bind with leather, 5000 copies for $3,000. Mr. Grandin got a new font of Small Pica, on which the body of the work was printed. When the printer was ready to commence work, Harris was notified, and Hyrum Smith brought the first installment of manuscript, of 24 pages, closely written on common foolscap paper—he had it under his vest, and vest and coat closely buttoned over it. At night Smith came and got the manuscript, and with the same precaution carried it away. The next morning with the same watchfulness, he brought it again, and at night took it away . . . Every Chapter, if I remember correctly, was one solid paragraph, without a punctuation mark, from beginning to end. Names of persons and places were generally capitalized, but sentences had no end . . . I punctuated it to make it read as I supposed the Author intended.[5]

While the work was in progress, a problem arose at the Grandin Bookstore when Abner Cole began publishing extracts from the Book of Mormon in his newspaper. After meeting with Hyrum Smith, Cole continued to work on pirating the Book of Mormon material. Joseph soon arrived from Harmony, Pennsylvania, and confronted him one Sunday afternoon. Cole was reminded of the copyright and asked not to continue his work. Joseph Smith's mother reported that at this point Cole threw off his coat, rolled up his sleeves, and came at Joseph smacking his fists together. "Do you want to fight, sir?" he demanded. Smiling, the young prophet asked Cole to put his coat back on. "It is cold, and I am not going to fight you," Joseph responded. "Sir," Cole challenged Joseph, "if you think you are the best man, just pull off your coat and try it."[6] Cole eventually cooled off and agreed to compromise. He shortly stopped running the extracts, but continued to print a commentary on the book and its publishers.

Missionary work began before the actual publication of the Book of Mormon was completed. Members of the Smith, Whitmer, and Cowdery families used proof sheets from the Book of Mormon in spreading the word in Wayne and adjoining counties. William Hyde, an early convert, recalled:

In the year 1830 . . . we began to hear something concerning the Book of Mormon, and the setting up of the Kingdom of God on earth in the last days. The little information that we gained upon this subject, until the Elders came preaching, was through Warren A. Cowdery, whose farm joined with ours. Warren A. obtained from his brother Oliver, at an early date, some of the proof sheets to the Book of Mormon some of which we had the privilege of perusing, and we did not peruse any faster than we believed.[7]

Rumors concerning the book spread throughout the area. Lucius Fenn of Convert, New York, wrote a letter to an old neighbor in Winchester, Connecticut on 12 February 1830. Along with the news items mentioned by Fenn, a book being printed at Palmyra, some fifty miles from Convert, was the news of the day. While local newspapers had been publishing advance notice of the book since early June 1829, Fenn's letter reveals how quickly the story had become common knowledge.

There is something that has taken place lately that is mysterious to us. It is this—there has been a bible found by 3 men but a short distance from us which is something remarkable we think. There was it is said an angel appeared to these 3 men and told them that there was a bible concealed in such a place and if one of them would go to that place he would find it . . . what is most wondered at is this, that the

Main Street, Palmyra, New York
(Including Grandin Building, the second building from the left)
Photograph courtesy of LDS Historical Dept.—Unknown, before 1910

man that found it could not read at all in the English language, but he
read this bible and nobody else cannot. It has been concealed there
for fourteen hundred years. It is written on a kind of gold leaf. It is
the same that ours is only there is an addition to it. They are printing
it in Palmyra.[8]

On 26 March 1830, Grandin published the title page of the Book
of Mormon in the *Wayne Sentinel* and announced, "The above work,
containing about 600 pages, large Deuodecimo, is now for sale, whole-
sale and retail, at the Palmyra Bookstore, by E. B. Grandin." The
publication of the book made Joseph a minor national figure as stories
about the book were published in other newspapers. Nevertheless, the
boycott organized in Palmyra was effective; and, as a result, Martin
Harris sold some of his farm to pay the printing costs that he had
obligated himself to earlier.

Surprisingly, the publication of the book did not elicit a lot of
comments from Joseph Smith or his family. The first edition made little mention of Joseph. The preface contained only one sentence about
his part in the work, and his own name appeared only on the title page
and in the testimony of the eight witnesses at the back. Seemingly,
Joseph presented the book to the world and moved on to other concerns — namely the organization of the Church in April.

On Tuesday, 6 April 1830, Joseph Smith and others met at Peter
Whitmer's farm in Fayette, New York, to organize legally the Church
of Christ. The group consisted of six elders and some fifty other individuals on the first Tuesday in April. This was a solemn but joyous
occasion. After services, which included prayer, singing, administration of the sacrament, and organizational matters, Joseph baptized
several individuals (including his father) and ordained others to the
priesthood.

Important as this meeting was to the future church, it was also
significant for the Smith family. For the first time, all living members
of the Smith household belonged to the same church. The occasion
was so emotional that Joseph's eyes filled with tears as he grasped his
father's hand during the baptism in a small stream near the farm home.
"Oh, my God! have I lived to see my own father baptized into the true
church of Jesus Christ!" Joseph Knight, a family friend and partici-
pant at this meeting, later recalled that Joseph "burst out with grief
and joy and [it] seemed as though the world could not hold him. He
went out into the lot (near the home) and appeared to want to get out

of sight of everybody and would sob and cry and seemed to be so full that he could not live." Knight finally went after him to bring him back to the home. "He was the most wrought upon that I ever saw any man," Knight recalled. "His joy seemed to be full."[9]

Originally, the translation of the Book of Mormon seemed to be the greatest work for Joseph; but eventually it became less an end in itself and more a means to bring people to Christ through the church that it foreshadowed. Lucy Mack Smith remembered,

> We communicated this intelligence to Martin Harris the same evening, for we loved the man . . . [W]hen he heard that the translation was finally completed, he seemed as greatly rejoiced as if he knew that it had affected his salvation, and determined to go straightway to Waterloo as soon as he could get away the next morning. We accordingly set off together, and before sunset we met Joseph and Oliver at Waterloo. The evening was past in reading the manuscript, and it would be superfluous for me to say to anyone who has read these pages that we were greatly rejoiced, for it had appeared to us . . . as though the greatest difficulty was then surmounted. But with Joseph it was not so, for he knew that a dispensation of the gospel was committed to him, of which the starting but had scarcely yet made its appearance.[10]

For Joseph, it was the Church and not the Book of Mormon that ultimately gave full expression to the call of repentance and reconciliation with God.

Immediately, these New York farmers and artisans began setting out to fill the earth with the good news. They began their work like the first disciples of Jesus. They had no allies or fellow workers and confronted a world that knew nothing of the message they were spreading. For Joseph, the older Christian churches were without authority, their works were dead, and the Mormons were alone to present the message of salvation to a fallen world.

In Palmyra, *The Reflector* stated that Oliver Cowdery, "Apostle to the Nephites," departed on a boat by way of the Erie Canal from Palmyra "with a load of Golden Bibles," to "declare the truth . . . in . . . principal cities of the Union." Samuel H. Smith, Joseph Smith's younger brother, left home with a knapsack full of Books of Mormon at the end of the month. Lucy Mack Smith recalled:

> On the 30th of June, Samuel started on the mission to which he had been set apart by Joseph, and in traveling twenty-five miles, which

Erie Canal, Rochester, New York
(Used by the missionaries and early Saints)
Photograph courtesy of Rochester Public Library — Unknown, unknown

was his first day's journey, he stopped at a number of places in order
to sell his books, but was turned out of doors as soon as he declared
his principles. When evening came on, he was faint and almost dis-
couraged, but coming to an inn, which was surrounded with every
appearance of plenty, he called to see if the landlord would buy one
of his books [he was turned out again] . . . Samuel was sick at heart,
for this was the fifth time he had been turned out of doors that day . . .
[H]e then proceeded five miles further on his journey, and seeing an
apple-tree a short distance from the road, he concluded to pass the
night under it; and here he lay all night upon the cold, damp ground.
In the morning he arose from his comfortless bed, and observing a
small cottage at no great distance, he drew near, hoping to get a little
refreshment. The only inmate was a widow, who seemed very poor.
He asked her for food, relating the story of his former treatment. She
prepared him some victuals, and, after eating, he explained to her
the history of the Book of Mormon. She listened attentively, and
believed all that he told her, but, in consequence of her poverty, she
was unable to purchase one of the books. He presented her with one,
and proceeded to Bloomington, which was eight miles further.[12]

Along with presenting the history of the Book of Mormon, many
early missionaries taught the basic doctrine of the Church. This basic
doctrine was presented in the form of a revelation.[13] This section,

known as the "Articles and Covenants," along with another revelation called the "Law of the Church,"[14] declared what the Church believed. With the Book of Mormon in hand and several handwritten copies of revelations, the missionaries spread across New York. These early revelations were eventually complied and printed in a book entitled The Doctrine and Covenants.

Joseph Smith not only intended to bring forth the Book of Mormon and a compilation of modern revelations but also a "translation" of the Bible. On 8 October 1829, Oliver Cowdery and Joseph Smith purchased a copy of a King James version of the Bible at the E.B. Grandin bookstore in Palmyra. This copy of the Bible was used by Joseph for his second major translation work, the Bible.[15]

Sometime in June 1830, just two months following the organization of the Church, Joseph Smith began a revision of the Bible in Colesville, New York. A revelation, the length of a bible chapter, was the introduction to his Bible translation. The rest of his work continued in the Book of Genesis. Following his move to Fayette, New York, Joseph continued his work; and by 1 December 1830 he had progressed as far as Genesis chapter six. While Joseph Smith was busy receiving revelations and working on his Bible translation, missionaries expanded their fields of labor.

Joseph Smith, Sr. had an important mission to perform himself. In Potsdam, a community located in the northeastern part of New York approximately thirty miles from the Canadian border, Joseph Sr. had family members living at the time. John Smith, his brother, apparently moved to Potsdam in 1805. By 1820, Asael and Mary Duty Smith and their six children had moved to the Stockholm and Potsdam area in St. Lawrence County. The family lived in the same area when in 1828 Joseph Smith, Sr. sent a letter to his father informing him of Joseph Jr.'s vision. Within two years, Joseph Smith, Sr. arrived in the Potsdam area with several copies of the newly published Book of Mormon. Eventually, Asael and Mary and three of the four surviving sons and all but two daughters were converted. Asael died the same year; and by 1836 Mary Duty Smith, along with Asael Jr., Silas, and John, gathered with the Saints in Ohio.

At an important conference held at Fayette, the usual business was preempted by a revelation calling for the Church to remove to Ohio. However, the revelation explained the reasons for such a move. The first reason for going, as everyone knew, was "that the enemy in the secret chambers seeketh your lives."[16] The second was the initiation

John Smith Home, Potsdam, New York
(Birthplace of George A. Smith in 1817)
Photograph from *Contributor* Vol. 12 (July 1908) —Edward H. Anderson, ca. 1908

Asael Smith Home, Winthrop, New York
(Asael Smith died here in 1830)
Photograph from *Contributor* Vol. 12 (Dec. 1908) —Edward H. Anderson, ca. 1908

of the gathering, "And that ye might escape the power of the enemy and be gathered unto me a righteous people, without spot and blameless—wherefore, for this cause I gave unto you the commandment that ye should go to the Ohio."[17] The Saints left their homes, farms, and businesses in New York not only to escape their enemies but also more importantly to search for the designated places where under the direction of their prophetic leader, Joseph Smith, they planned to build the City of God and to establish Zion in a promised land.

In 1831, three separate groups of Saints left New York and headed west to Ohio. These groups traveled along the Erie Canal from Palmyra to Rochester. At South Street in modern Rochester, the street crosses the Genesee River right on top of the original 802-foot-long aqueduct that carried the canal across the river.

From Rochester, the Saints traveled another sixty miles to Lockport. Between Montezuma and Buffalo, the boats were raised almost 180 feet by various locks in the canal. At Lockport, a series of five separate locks were used to raise the canal boats fifty-six feet. The route from Lockport was southwest until the boats reached the Niagara River, where they traveled south to Buffalo Harbor. At Buffalo, the Saints made passages on Lake Erie steamers to Ohio.

Mormon activity did not come to an end in New York after the departure of the Saints to Ohio in 1831. Several missionary and business trips were conducted by Church leaders and missionaries during the first decades following the organization of the Church in 1830. In

First Aqueduct over Genesee River, Rochester, New York
(Part of the Erie Canal which was used by the Saints)
Drawing courtesy of Rochester Public Library—W.H.S., 1828

1832, several missionaries left Kirtland for points east, including New York. By year's end, Martin Harris and Emer Harris had baptized one hundred at Chenango Point, New York. Several of the Twelve embarked on a steamer at Fairport, Ohio, for Dunkirk, New York, and on 9 May 1832 organized branches of the Church at Westfield, Silver Creek, Perrysburg, and Lavona at the Westfield Conference. On 22 May, they organized the Freedom Conference, comprising numerous branches of the Church in the area.

In March 1832, the United Order, or United Firm, a business partnership organized to consolidate business activity for the benefit of the Church, was established. Sidney Gilbert and Newel K. Whitney were assigned as agents of the firm in Missouri and Ohio. As a result of instruction received on 22-23 September 1832, Joseph Smith, along with N. K. Whitney, began a trip to New York City. The revelation stated,

> And the bishop, Newel K. Whitney, also should travel round about and among all the churches, searching after the poor to administer to their wants by humbling the rich and the proud. He should also employ an agent to take charge and to do his secular business as he shall direct. Nevertheless, let the bishop go unto the city of New York, also to the city of Albany, and also to the city of Boston, and warn the people of those cities with the sound of the gospel, with a loud voice, of desolation and utter abolishment which await them if they do reject these things.[18]

Joseph and Newel arrived in New York City on 13 October 1832 and resided at the Pearl Street House, a boarding house located at 88 Pearl Street near the southern end of Manhattan Island. The house was located in the heart of the city's commercial district. At the time, New York City had a population of some two hundred thousand people. While in New York City, Whitney stated, "We visited Bishop [Benjamin T.] Onderdonk of the Episcopal Church of the United States . . . "[19] Joseph Smith wrote his wife, Emma, on the same day of their arrival as follows:

> October 13, 1832
> Pearl Street House New York
>
> My Dear Wife
>
> This day I have been walking through the most splendid part of the City of New York. The buildings are truly great and wonderful to

Pearl Street, New York City, New York
(Pearl Street House where Church leaders stayed in 1832)
Drawing courtesy of the New York Historical Society — M. Osborne, 1831

the astonishment of every beholder and the language of my heart is like this, Can the great God of all the Earth maker of all things magnificent and splendid be displeased with man for all these great inventions sought out by them. My answer is not, it can not be seeing these works are calculated to make men comfortable wise and happy, therefore not for the works can the Lord be displeased. Against man is the anger of the Lord kindled because they give him not the glory therefore their iniquities shall be visited upon their heads and their works shall be burned up ... There is about one hundred boarders and sometimes more in this house every day from one to two from all parts of the world. I think you would have laughed right hearty if you could have been here. You could see the waiters today at noon as they waited on the table both black and white and mulatto running, bowing, and maneuvering. But I must conclude, I remain your affectionate husband until death.[20]

A year later, Joseph Smith left Kirtland for Upper Canada, which took him through the state of New York. He left Kirtland on 5 October 1833 on a "preaching journey." His party arrived at the home of Elder Nickerson in Perrysburg, Cattaraugus County, New York, soon thereafter. On Saturday, 12 October, Joseph Smith recorded,

> Saturday the 12th the house of the Father Nickerson. I feel very well in my mind the Lord is with us, but I have much anxiety about my family etc. Sunday the 13th held a meeting at Freeman Nickerson's

had a large congregation Brother Sidney preached and I bore record to the people the Lord gave his spirit in a marvelous manner for which I am thankful to the God of Abraham Lord bless my family and preserve them. Monday 14th at the same place this day expect to start for Canada Lord be with us on our journey Amen.[21]

A revelation known as LDS D&C 100/RLDS D&C 97 was given in Perrysburg, New York, as a result of Joseph's anxiety about his family. John P. Greene, who met Joseph at Father Nickerson's home, recorded,

> I went to Brother Nickerson's in Perrysburg and met Brothers Joseph Smith and Sidney Rigdon. Sidney preached in the demonstration of the spirit and afterwards I . . . spent the evening with the Brethren with grate satisfaction in company with Joseph.[22]

The revelation informed both Joseph and Sidney that "your families are well; they are in my hands, and I will do with them as seemeth me good; for in me there is all power." They were informed further that the Lord "had much people in this place, in the regions round about; and an effectual door shall be opened in the regions round about

Campbell-Vail Hotel, Perrysburg, New York
(1828 Hotel stood here when Church leaders visited in 1833)
Photograph courtesy of Perrysburg Historical Society — Unknown, unknown

in this eastern land. Therefore, I, the Lord, have suffered you to come unto this place; for thus it was expedient in me for the salvation of souls."[23] Several branches were eventually organized in the area, including Freedom, which was the home of Oliver Cowdery's bother, Warren.

In 1834, on a trip to obtain volunteers for Zion's Camp, Joseph Smith visited many of these same villages and towns. In Perrysburg, Joseph stayed with Vincent Knight on 22 March 1834 and Father Nickerson on 23 March.

Other missionaries traveled through New York to their mission fields farther east or north. Parley P. Pratt had been called to "Upper Canada, even to the city of Toronto, the capital, and there thou shalt find a people prepared for the fulness of the gospel, and they shall receive thee, and thou shalt organize the Church among them."[24] Leaving Kirtland with Brother Nickerson, they traveled in a public coach, since the lake was not open yet. Pratt recorded that it was a "long and tedious passage in a public coach, the roads being very bad . . . we arrived at the Falls of Niagara sometime in the month of April 1836."[25] The falls were an awe-inspiring sight for Pratt, who wrote:

> We halted a short time to view this wonder of nature, and to adore that God who had formed a world so sublimely grand. The leaping of a mighty river of waters over a perpendicular fall of one hundred and sixty feet, the foaming and dashing of its white spray upon the rocks beneath; the rising cloud of mist with its glittering rainbow, the yawning gulf with its thousand whirlpools; all conspired to fill the contemplative mind with wonder and admiration, and with reverence to the Great Author of all the wonders of creation; while its everlasting roar which may be heard for many miles distant, seemed a lively emblem of eternity.[26]

The moment at Niagara triggered Pratt's poetic impulse. He wrote:

> O, Niagara! Generations may pass in long succession; ages may roll away and others still succeed; empires may rise and flourish, and pass away and be forgotten; but still thy deafening, thy solemn and awful voice is heard in one eternal roar.
>
> The temples of marble may moulder to dust, the monuments of the great may crumble to decay, the palaces of kings fall to ruin and their very place become unknown, their history forgotten in the almost countless ages of antiquity, and still thy sound is heard in everlasting moan, as if mourning over the ruins of by-gone years.[27]

Niagara Falls, Niagara, New York
(Parley P. Pratt visited here in 1836)
Photo courtesy of Buffalo and Erie County Historical Society — Unknown, ca. 1868

While Pratt and others passed through New York on their way to prospective mission areas, other LDS missionaries stopped in New York to reintroduce the message.

Among those New Yorkers who heard the Mormon message and responded to it was Zina Diantha Huntington Young. During her youth in New York, Zina recalled,

> In my earliest reading of history, Confucius, Columbus, and William Wallace, I used to muse while watching the consuming back log

in our old fashion fireplace why I could not have been born in a day when something was going on in the nations of the Earth, not that I wished to see distress, but some enterprise.[28]

Unbeknownst to the daughter of a prosperous New York farmer, however, was that at the very moment she lay musing over these things, something was "going on"; and an "enterprise" was beginning to take place that would forever change her life and the religious history of the state of New York.

Zina's father, Willington Huntington, left the Presbyterian faith and joined the Congregationalist following a controversy over the method of appointing clergy in the church. At the time, news regarding a "Golden Bible," often in the form of rumors, spread in the area of Watertown, New York, where the Huntington family lived. One hundred miles from Watertown, in Palmyra, Joseph Smith had published the Book of Mormon. A family friend, Joseph Wakefield, left to visit the "new" prophet and returned with a report to Zina's father. He brought with him a copy of the "Golden Bible."

Zina remembered, "One day on my return from school I saw the Book of Mormon, that strange, new book, lying on the window sill of our sitting-room. I went up to the window, picked it up, and the sweet influence of the Holy Spirit accompanied, it to such an extent that I pressed it to my bosom in a rapture of delight, murmuring as I did so, 'This is the truth, truth, truth.'"[29] After a visit by Hyrum Smith and David Whitmer to her home, she joined the new church at fourteen years of age.

New York was not only the birthplace of Mormonism itself but also the birthplace of several Saints, including W. W. Blair, Jason Briggs, Zebedee Coltrin, Jedediah M. Grant, Martin Harris, Lydia G. Knight, John E. Page, David W. Patten, Parley P. Pratt, George A. Smith, John Van Cott, Daniel H. Wells, and Helen Mar Whitney.

Buffalo, New York

Buffalo is located in the northwestern part of the state, is situated on the Canadian border, and is at the east end of Lake Erie.

White settlement began when the French established a small settlement in 1758, which the British burned just a year later. In 1800, Joseph Ellicot arrived to inform the settlers who remained after the

Buffalo, New York
(Important commercial center in the 1830s)
Photo courtesy of Buffalo and Erie County Historical Society — Unknown, ca. 1870

British burning that the Holland Land Company was the owner of the land; and he proceeded to map out "New Amsterdam." The local inhabitants called the town Buffalo instead. The town continued to grow until it was burned again by British forces during the War of 1812.

Citizens rallied and rebuilt the town and in 1818 constructed the first Great Lakes steamboat, *Walk-on-the-Water*. This event, along with the completion of the Erie Canal, turned the small village of Buffalo into an important city by 1825. Buffalo became the nucleus of the shipping-trade business among the Great Lakes region, Canada, and the eastern United States.

The Saints traveled through Buffalo beginning with the first missionary trek west by Oliver Cowdery, Parley P. Pratt, Ziba Peterson, and Peter Whitmer in 1830. Soon, many of the New York Saints arrived in Buffalo on their way to the new Church gathering place in Ohio. Thereafter, Buffalo was a standard stop for Church leaders, businessmen, and missionaries on their way to the eastern part of the United

Buffalo Harbor, Buffalo, New York
(Several groups of Saints left New York from here in 1831)
Photo courtesy of Buffalo and Erie County Historical Society — Unknown, 1867

States. Lucy Mack Smith described the events at Buffalo in 1831 as follows:

> [We] arrived at Buffalo on the fifth day after leaving Waterloo. Here we found the brethren from Colesville, who informed us that they had been detained one week in this place, waiting for navigation to open.

Soon thereafter, Lucy Mack Smith continued,

> I said, "Now brethren and sisters, if you will all of you raise your desires to heaven, that the ice may be broken up, and we be set at liberty, as sure as the Lord lives it will be done." At that instant a noise was heard, like bursting thunder. The captain cried, "Every man to his post." The ice parted, leaving barely a passage for the boat, and so narrow, that, as the boat passed through, the buckets of the water-wheel were torn off with a crash, which, joined to the word of command from the captain, the hoarse answering of the sailors, the noise of the ice, and the cries and confusion of the spectators, presented a scene truly terrible. We had barely passed through the avenue, when the ice closed together again, and the Colesville

brethren were left in Buffalo, unable to follow us. As we were leaving the harbor, one of the bystanders explained, "there goes the Mormons company! That boat is sunk in the water nine inches deeper than ever it was before and, mark it, she will sink — there is nothing surer." In fact, they were so sure of it that they went straight to the office and had it published that we sunk, so that when we arrived at Fairport, we read in the papers the news of our own death. After our miraculous escape from the wharf at Buffalo, we called our company together, and had a prayer-meeting, in which we offered up our thanks to God for his mercy, which he had manifested towards us in our deliverance.[30]

Manchester, New York

Manchester is located near to the New York State Thruway (Exit 43), and is approximately twenty-eight miles east of Rochester.

During the summer of 1789, the Comstock family (consisting of a father and his two sons) built a log cabin and prepared four acres of land for wheat in the northern section of the town of Farmington, a few miles west of the Smith farm. Several others migrated to the area the same year. Ezra and Stephen Phelps settled near the Hill Cumorah. The New York State Legislature organized Ontario County; and by 1790, four townships existed, including Palmyra and Farmington. At this time, Robert Robinson purchased part of the Phelps farm, which included the Hill Cumorah. Farmington was later divided in 1821, and the second section was named Burt. Eventually, in 1822, it was renamed Manchester Town.

SMITH FAMILY LOG CABIN SITE *(Palmyra)*

The Smith log cabin site is located on Stafford Road approximately two miles from the Palmyra town center. The site is about 250 yards north of the present Joseph Smith, Sr. house. The cabin site was situated on the west side of the road, just over the Manchester township line in Palmyra township.

Historical Background

Many of the original buildings of the Smith farm are no longer standing, such as the barn, cooper's (barrel-making) shop, apple orchard, hand–split rail fences, and the first Smith home, the old log cabin. The cabin was located right across the Manchester township line and therefore was located in Palmyra township.

Some of the most significant events in Church history occurred while Joseph Sr. and Lucy Smith lived in this cabin. They were living there when the First Vision occurred, when Moroni visited young Joseph for the first time in 1823, when the eight witnesses saw the plates, and when the Book of Mormon was printed in Palmyra.

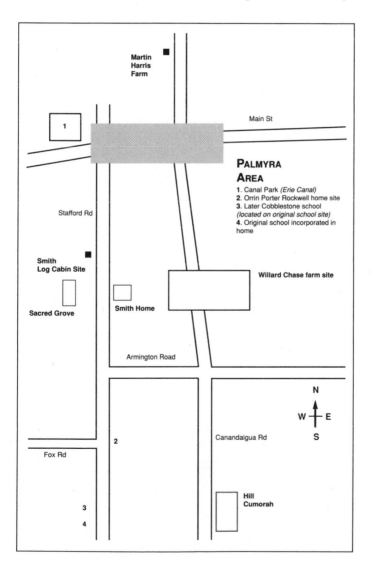

Martin Harris Farm

Main St

PALMYRA AREA
1. Canal Park *(Erie Canal)*
2. Orrin Porter Rockwell home site
3. Later Cobblestone school *(located on original school site)*
4. Original school incorporated in home

Stafford Rd

Smith Log Cabin Site

Willard Chase farm site

Sacred Grove

Smith Home

Armington Road

N
W ─┼─ E
S

Canandaigua Rd

Fox Rd

Hill Cumorah

The cabin stood a few hundred feet north and west across the road from where the frame house stands today. The cabin was built by Father Smith and his sons. Of all the houses they lived in, Lucy felt this log cabin was the epitome of home:

> Two years from the time we entered Palmyra, strangers, destitute of friends or home or employment, we were able to settle ourselves upon our own land, in a snug comfortable though humble habitation built and neatly furnished by our own industry . . . [one and half stories] a garret above divided into two apartments. (Its foundation measured approximately twenty-four by thirty feet.)[31]

Aerial Photograph, Palmyra, New York
(Site of Smith Farm, Hill Cumorah, Palmyra and Harris Farm)
Photograph courtesy USDA-ASCS Aerial Photography — Unknown, 1954

JOSEPH SMITH, SR. HOME

The Joseph Smith, Sr. farm house is located on the east side of Stafford Road approximately two miles south of the Palmyra town center.

Historical Background

The Smiths lived in their log home from late 1818 until spring 1825 and from spring 1829 to late 1830. From 1825 to 1829, the Smiths lived in a white frame home. Lucy Mack Smith mentions the construction of this home as follows:

> We were still making arrangements to build us a comfortable house, the management and control of which evolved chiefly upon Alvin. And when Nov. 1822 arrived, the frame was raised, and all the materials necessary for its speedy completion were procured. This opened to Alvin's mind the pleasing prospect of seeing his father and mother to sit in, and everything arranged for their comfort, and they shall not work any more as they have done.[32]

Aerial Photograph, Manchester, New York
(Joseph Smith, Sr. Farm — log cabin site right side)
Photograph courtesy of LDS Visual Resources Library — Craig W. Dimond, 1988

Joseph Smith, Sr. Farm, Manchester, New York
(Eight witnesses viewed plates here in 1829)
Photograph courtesy of LDS Historical Dept. — George E. Anderson, 1907

The home did more than provide a comfortable habitat for the Smiths. It also was the scene of some important events concerning the Book of Mormon. Shortly after Joseph obtained the record in 1827, he brought it back to the home to hide it. Lucy recalled this event in her personal history:

> After resting a few moments, he desired me to send Carlos . . . to Hyrum's, to tell him to bring the chest . . . When the chest came, Joseph locked up the Record, then threw himself upon the bed . . . Shortly after this circumstance, Joseph . . . determined that a portion of the hearth should be taken up, and the Record and breast-plate should be buried under the same, and then the hearth be re-laid, to prevent suspicion. This was done as speedily as possible, but the hearth was scarcely re-laid when a large company of men well armed came rushing up to the house. Joseph threw open the doors, and taking a hint from the stratagem of his grandfather Mack, hallooed as if had a legion at hand, in the meanwhile, giving the word of command with great emphasis; while all the male portion of the family, from the father down to little Carlos, ran out of the house with such fury upon the mob, that it struck them with terror and dismay, and they fled before the little Spartan band into the woods.[33]

After the Smith family lost their farm in Manchester, Joseph Smith, Sr. moved the family just two miles east of Kingdom Village, near Fayette, in 1830. Lucy Mack Smith recalled,

Joseph Smith, Sr. Home, Manchester, New York
(Built by the Smith sons for their parents)
Photograph courtesy of Margaret Rich — Unknown, ca. 1910

We moved into a house belonging to an individual by the name of
Kellogg. Shortly after arriving here, we were made to realize that
the hearts of the people were in the hands of the Lord; for we had
scarcely unpacked our goods when one of our new neighbors, a Mr.
Osgood, came in and invited us to drive our stock and teams to his
barn-yard, and feed them from his barn, free of cost, until we could
make further arrangements. Many of our neighbors came in, and
welcomed us to Waterloo. Among whom was Mr. Hooper, a tavern-
keeper, whose wife came with him, and brought us a present of
some delicate eatables. Such manifestations of kindness as these were
shown to us from day to day, during our continuance in the place.
And they were duly appreciated, for we had experienced the opposite so severely that the least show of good feeling gave rise to the
liveliest sensations of gratitude. Having settled ourselves in this place,
we established the practice of spending the evenings in singing and
praying. The neighbors soon became aware of this, and it caused our
house to become a place of evening resort for some dozen or twenty
persons.[34]

THE SACRED GROVE

The Sacred Grove is located across Stafford Road approximately one-fourth mile from the Joseph Smith, Sr. farm house.

Aerial Photograph, Manchester, New York
(Identified as the Sacred Grove — lower portion)
Photograph courtesy of LDS Visual Resources Library — Craig W. Dimond, 1988

Historic Background

Joseph related and wrote about his vision on several occasions. Each story contributes to a larger understanding of what happened and what the vision meant to the young boy as he matured and as the work of restoration continued. He had been seriously interested in religion as early as 1817 or 1818. During this period of confusion, he came across a New Testament passage, "If any of you lack wisdom, let him ask of God that giveth to all men liberally . . . and it shall be given." (James 1:5) "Never did any passage of scripture," Joseph later wrote, "come with more power to the heart of man than this did at

Sacred Grove, Manchester, New York
(Father and Son appeared here in 1820)
Photograph courtesy of LDS Historical Dept. — George E. Anderson, 1907

this time to mine. It seemed to enter with great force into every feeling of my heart. I reflected on it again and again."[35]

> Information was what I most desired at this time, and with a fixed determination to obtain it, I called on the Lord for the first time in the place above stated, or in other words, I made a fruitless attempt to pray. My tongue seemed to be swollen in my mouth, so that I could not utter, I heard a noise behind me like some one walking towards me. I strove again to pray, but could not; the noise of walking seemed to draw nearer, I sprang upon my feet and looked round, but saw no person or thing that was calculated to produce the noise of walking. I kneeled again, my mouth was opened and my tongue loosed; I called on the Lord in mighty prayer. A pillar of fire appeared above my head; which presently rested down upon me, and filled me with unspeakable joy. A personage appeared in the midst of this pillar of flame, which was spread all around and yet nothing consumed. Another personage soon appeared like unto the first he said unto me thy sins are forgiven thee. He testified also unto me that Jesus Christ is the son of God. I saw many angels in this vision.[36]

Several years later, in a letter to John Wentworth, a newspaper publisher in Chicago, Joseph wrote this:

Joseph Smith, Sr. Farm, Manchester, New York
(Stream between the Smith Home and the Sacred Grove)
Photograph courtesy of LDS Historical Dept. — George E. Anderson, 1907

Believing the word of God I had confidence in the declaration of James, "If any man lack wisdom let him ask of God who giveth to all men liberally and upbraideth not and it shall be given him," I retired to a secret place in a grove and began to call upon the Lord, while fervently engaged in supplication my mind was taken away from the objects with which I was surrounded, and I was enwrapped in a heavenly vision and saw two glorious personages who exactly resembled each other in features, and likeness, surrounded with a brilliant light which eclipsed the sun at noon-day. They told me that all religious denominations were believing in incorrect doctrines, and that none of them was acknowledged of God as his church and kingdom. And I was expressly commanded to "go not after them," at the same time receiving a promise that the fulness of the gospel would at some future time be made known unto me. [37]

DISTRICT SCHOOL SITE *(Cobble Stone)*

The district school site is located on the west side of Stafford Road approximately one mile south of the intersection of Stafford and Armington roads. The district school house was situated on the site presently occupied by the later cobblestone school house. The earlier

District School Site, Manchester, New York
(Smith family children attended here)
Photograph courtesy of the authors—Richard Neitzel Holzapfel, 1990

District School House, Manchester, New York
(Oliver Cowdery taught here)
Photograph courtesy of the authors — T. Jeffery Cottle, 1990

frame school house (of Joseph's day) was moved and incorporated into the house directly south of the cobblestone school house.

Historical Background

During the critical period of 1827, an important contact was made in Manchester between the Smith family and an individual who would eventually play an important role in the restoration. Lucy Mack Smith wrote,

> A man by the name of Lyman Cowdery came into the neighborhood, and applied to Hyrum, (as he was one of the trustees,) for the district school. A meeting was called, and Mr. Cowdery was employed. But the following day, this Mr. Cowdery brought his brother Oliver to the trustees, and requested them to receive him instead of himself, as circumstances had transpired which rendered it necessary for him to disappoint them, or which would not allow of his attending to the school himself; and he would warrant that to the good conduct of the school under his brother's supervision. All parties being satisfied, Oliver commenced his school, boarding for the time being at our house. He had been in the school but a short time, when he began to hear from all quarters concerning the plates, and as soon began to importune Mr. Smith upon the subject, but for

Old Quaker Meeting Hall, Farmington, New York
(Early meeting hall in use in 1820)
Photograph courtesy of Milton V. Backman—Milton V. Backman, Jr., 1970

a considerable length of time did not succeed in eliciting any information. At last, however, he gained my husband's confidence, so far as to obtain a sketch of the facts relative to the plates.[38]

THE HILL CUMORAH

The Hill Cumorah is located on the east side of Canandaigua Road approximately two miles north from the New York State Thruway (Exit 43). An LDS Visitors Center is also located here.

Historical Background

The visitation of the Angel Moroni to Joseph Smith on the night of 21–22 September 1823 signaled the unique foundation of Mormonism. A statue representing Moroni (10' 4" tall) crowns the hill now known as Cumorah. The dedicatory program for the Angel Moroni Monument occurred on 21 July 1935. In one hand, the figure holds plates symbolic of the Book of Mormon, the ancient religious record whose existence was revealed to Joseph Smith by Moroni.

On the west slope of the hill, Smith found a large, rounded stone. Underneath, he discovered a stone box containing the plates and an instrument later used to aid in translation. The instrument apparently consisted of two transparent stones identified by the angel as a device used by ancient seers. After annual visits to the hill, Joseph finally obtained the plates in the fall of 1827. Joseph wrote in 1832 the following account of those events:

> I was seventeen years of age I called again upon the Lord and he shewed unto me a heavenly vision for behold an angel of the Lord came and stood before me and it was by night and he called me by name and he said the Lord had forgiven me my sins and he revealed unto me that in the Town of Manchester Ontario County N.Y. there was plates of gold upon which there was engravings which was engraven by Moroni & his fathers the servants of the living God in ancient days and deposited by the commandments of God and kept by the power thereof and that I should go and get them and he revealed unto me many things concerning the inhabitants of the earth which since have been revealed in commandments and revelations and it was on the 22d day of Sept. AD 1822 and thus he appeared unto me three times in one night and once on the next day and then I

Aerial Photograph, Manchester, New York
(Hill Cumorah — lower right)
Photograph courtesy of LDS Visual Resource Library — Craig W. Dimond, 1988

immediately went to the place and found where the plates was deposited as the angel of the Lord had commanded me and straightway made three attempts to get them and then being exceedingly frightened I supposed it had been a dream or Vision but when I considered I knew that it was not therefore I cried unto the Lord in the agony of my soul why can I not obtain them behold the angel appeared unto me again and said unto me you have not kept the commandments of the Lord which I gave unto you therefore you cannot now obtain them for the time is not yet fulfilled therefore thou wast left unto temptation that thou mightest be made acquainted with the power of the adversary therefore repent and call on the Lord thou shalt be forgiven and in his own due time thou shalt obtain them for now I had been tempted of the adversary and sought the Plates to obtain riches and kept not the commandment that I should have an eye single to the glory of God therefore I was chastened and sought diligently to obtain the plates and obtained them not until I was twenty one years of age.[39]

After the Book of Mormon was published, the Hill Cumorah was also called "Mormon Hill," "Bible Hill," and the "Golden Bible Hill"— all reflecting a distinct association with the Book of Mormon.[40]

Hill Cumorah, Manchester, New York
(Joseph Smith, Jr. obtained the plates here in 1827)
Photograph courtesy of LDS Historical Dept. — George E. Anderson, 1907

Oliver Cowdery visited the hill in 1830, and he provided an excellent and detailed description of the hill and the approximate location where the plates were deposited:

> The hill of which I have been speaking, at the time mentioned, presented a varied appearance: the north end rose suddenly from the plain, forming a promontory without timber, but covered with grass. As you passed to the south you soon came to scattering timber, the surface having been cleared by art or by wind; and a short distance further left, you are surrounded with the common forest of the country. It is necessary to observe, that even the part cleared was only occupied for pasturage its steep ascent and narrow summit not admitting the plow of the husbandman, with any degree of ease or profit. It was at the second mentioned place where the record was found to be deposited, on the west side of the hill, not far from the top down its side; and when myself visited the place in the 1830, there were several trees standing: enough to cause a shade in summer, but not so much as to prevent the surface being covered with grass—which was also the case when the record was first found.[41]

In 1831, a newspaper correspondent for the *Christian Register* also described the features of the Hill Cumorah:

> This hill has since been called by some, the Golden Bible Hill. The road from Canandaigua to Palmyra runs along its western base, at the northern extremity the hill is quite abrupt and narrow. It runs to the south for half a mile and then spreads out into a piece of broad table lane, covered with beautiful orchards and wheat fields . . . It is profusely covered to the top with Beach, Maple, Bass, and Whitewood the northern extremity is quite bare of trees.[42]

Palmyra, New York

Palmyra is located approximately twenty-eight miles east of Rochester, New York, and is about six miles north on the Canandaigua Road from the New York State Thruway (Exit 43).

The interior of New York was controlled by the Iroquois confederation, a group of six Indian tribes. During the Revolutionary War, the Iroquois were caught in the struggle and, as a result, suffered the consequences of the fighting. In 1779, General John Sullivan attacked the Seneca tribes and destroyed their fields, orchards, and

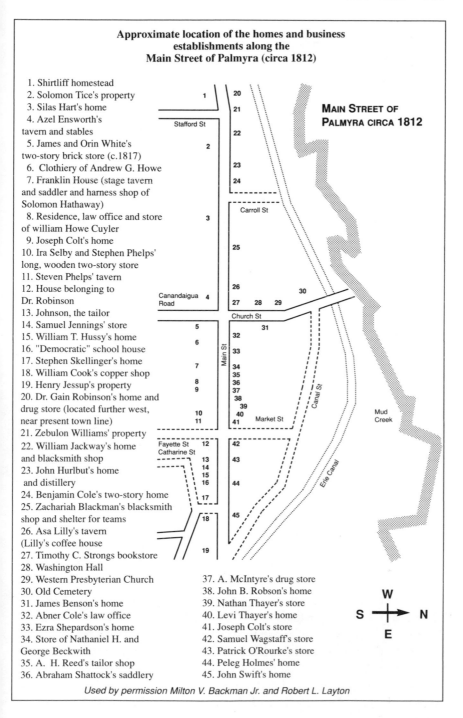

**Approximate location of the homes and business
establishments along the
Main Street of Palmyra (circa 1812)**

1. Shirtliff homestead
2. Solomon Tice's property
3. Silas Hart's home
4. Azel Ensworth's
tavern and stables
5. James and Orin White's
two-story brick store (c.1817)
6. Clothiery of Andrew G. Howe
7. Franklin House (stage tavern
and saddler and harness shop of
Solomon Hathaway)
8. Residence, law office and store
of william Howe Cuyler
9. Joseph Colt's home
10. Ira Selby and Stephen Phelps'
long, wooden two-story store
11. Steven Phelps' tavern
12. House belonging to
Dr. Robinson
13. Johnson, the tailor
14. Samuel Jennings' store
15. William T. Hussy's home
16. "Democratic" school house
17. Stephen Skellinger's home
18. William Cook's copper shop
19. Henry Jessup's property
20. Dr. Gain Robinson's home and
drug store (located further west,
near present town line)
21. Zebulon Williams' property
22. William Jackway's home
and blacksmith shop
23. John Hurlbut's home
and distillery
24. Benjamin Cole's two-story home
25. Zachariah Blackman's blacksmith
shop and shelter for teams
26. Asa Lilly's tavern
(Lilly's coffee house
27. Timothy C. Strongs bookstore
28. Washington Hall
29. Western Presbyterian Church
30. Old Cemetery
31. James Benson's home
32. Abner Cole's law office
33. Ezra Shepardson's home
34. Store of Nathaniel H. and
George Beckwith
35. A. H. Reed's tailor shop
36. Abraham Shattock's saddlery

37. A. McIntyre's drug store
38. John B. Robson's home
39. Nathan Thayer's store
40. Levi Thayer's home
41. Joseph Colt's store
42. Samuel Wagstaff's store
43. Patrick O'Rourke's store
44. Peleg Holmes' home
45. John Swift's home

**MAIN STREET OF
PALMYRA CIRCA 1812**

Stafford St

Carroll St

Canandaigua
Road

Church St

Main St

Canal St

Erie Canal

Mud
Creek

Market St

Fayette St
Catharine St

W
S —┼— N
E

Used by permission Milton V. Backman Jr. and Robert L. Layton

homes. More than forty villages were either evacuated or destroyed by Sullivan's American troops. The troops publicized the fact that western New York contained beautiful lakes, forests, and choice farm land. To stimulate migration to the area, Oliver Phelps sent several expeditions into the region as early as 1788. Soon, the New York Legislature created Ontario County, named after the great lake that originally formed its northern boundary. By 1790, Ontario County was divided into four townships; and, in 1800, nineteen towns were located there.

Palmyra was created during this period and consisted of an area six miles by twelve miles. When Wayne County was created, Palmyra was divided into two townships: the western half was named Macedon, and the eastern half retained the name of Palmyra. Just south of Palmyra was another township, Farmington. Farmington was divided in 1821, and the second section was named Burt but eventually was renamed Manchester Town in 1822.

E. B. GRANDIN BOOK STORE

The E. B. Grandin Book Store is located in the village of Palmyra. From the intersection of Main and Church Streets, the bookstore is situated about 0.2 of a mile east on Main.

Historical Background

E. B. Grandin was born on 30 March 1806 in Frechold, Monmouth County, New Jersey. He married Harriet Rogers on 23 December in Palmyra, New York. Grandin bought his Palmyra printing business and bookstore in 1827 from John H. Gilbert. Sometime before 1833, Grandin left the printing business. He died 16 April 1845 in Pultneyville, New York.

"The printing was done," John Gilbert recalled, "in the third story of the west end of 'Exchange Row,' and the binding by Mr. Howard, in the second story, the lower story being used as a book store, by Mr. Grandin."

After contracting with Grandin for publication of the Book of Mormon, Joseph had Oliver Cowdery make a second copy, known as the printer's copy. This second copy was delivered to Grandin with little punctuation or paragraphing. The Grandin building was used on Sundays and evenings by Abner Cole, editor and proprietor of *The Reflector*. He published under the pseudonym of O. Dogberry. Beginning with the 2 January 1830 issue and continuing in the 13 and 22

E.B. Grandin Building, Palmyra, New York
(Book of Mormon was printed here in 1830)
Photograph courtesy of LDS Historical Dept. — Unknown, before 1920

January issues, Cole printed sections from 1 Nephi and Alma. After discovering that Cole was illegally printing these abstracts, Joseph Smith traveled from his home in Harmony, Pennsylvania, to Palmyra and threatened legal action against Cole unless Cole stopped. In one of his first comments on the book, Cole wrote:

> The Book, when it shall come forth before the public must stand or fall, according to the whims and fancies of its readers. How it will stand the test of criticism, we are not prepared to say, not having as yet examined many of its pages. — We are, however, prepared to state that from part of the first chapter, now before us, and which we this day publish, we cannot discover anything treasonable, or which will have a tendency to subvert our liberties. As to its religious character, we have as yet no means of determining, and if we had, we should be quite loth to meddle with the tender conscience of our neighbors.[44]

Grandin's journal, which begins in January 1831, records the events on 14 July 1831 as follows:

> In Bookstore some of the time. Spent most of the day in moving Gold Bibles from Mr. Howard's Bindery to my Bookstore. Weather cool, some rain.[45]

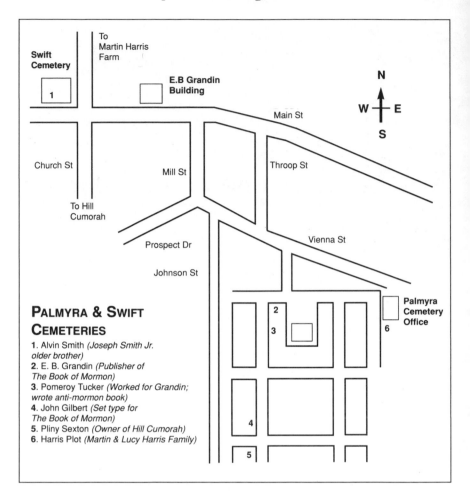

JOHN SWIFT MEMORIAL CEMETERY

The John Swift Memorial Cemetery is located on the west side of Church Street approximately two hundred yards north of the intersection of Church and Main Streets. The original Palmyra school house and church were also located in the vicinity of the Memorial Cemetery.

Historical Background
Alvin Smith was born on 11 February 1799 at Tunbridge, Orange County, Vermont. He died on 19 November 1823 at Palmyra, Ontario County, New York. Alvin was buried in the John Swift Memorial Cemetery. After rumors spread that Alvin's body had been exhumed

Alvin Smith Tombstone, Palmyra, New York
(Joseph Smith's older brother died in 1823)
Photograph courtesy of LDS Historical Dept. — Unknown, unknown

and dissected, Joseph Smith, Sr. and several others dug into the grave on 30 September 1824 and found the body to be undisturbed.

The following announcement concerning this incident appeared in the *Wayne Sentinel*:

> To the Public. Whereas reports have been industriously put in circulation, that my son Alvin had been removed from the place of his interment and dissected, which reports, every person possessed of human sensibility must know, are peculiarly calculated to harrow up the mind of a parent and deeply wound the feelings of relations — therefore, for the purpose of ascertaining the truth of such reports, I, with some of my neighbors, this morning repaired to the grave, and removing the earth, found the body which had not been disturbed. This method is taken for the purpose of satisfying the minds of those who may have heard the report, and of informing those who have put it in circulation, that it is earnestly requested they would desist

there from; and that it is believed by some, that they have been stimulated more by a desire to injure the reputation of certain persons than philanthropy for the peace and welfare of myself and friends. JOSEPH SMITH Palmyra, Sept. 25th, 1824[46]

The tombstone reads, "In memory of Alvin, son of Joseph and Lucy Smith, who died Nov. 19, 1823 in the 25th year of his life."

PALMYRA CEMETERY

The Palmyra Cemetery is located southeast of the town of Palmyra. The cemetery is located on the south side of Vienna Street just east of Johnson Street.

Historical Background
The tombstones of several individuals closely related to the founding of Mormonism are located in this cemetery. They include E. B. Grandin (printer of the Book of Mormon), Pomeroy Tucker (worked for E. B. Grandin and wrote an early anti-Mormon book), Pliny Sexton (owner of the Hill Cumorah), the Harris family plot (Martin and Lucy Harris family), and John H. Gilbert (typesetter for the Book of Mormon).

John H. Gilbert, Jr. Tombstone, Palmyra, New York
(Typesetter and pressman at E.B. Grandin Bookstore)
Photograph courtesy of Susan Easton Black — Susan Easton Black, 1990

Gilbert gave the following statement in Palmyra, New York, on 23 October 1887:

> I assisted E. B. Grandin in estimating the expense of printing 5000 copies of the Mormon Bible, and the price agreed upon was $3000. I was the principal compositor of said Bible, commencing on the same in August 1829 and finishing the same in March, 1830. John H. Gilbert[47]

MARTIN HARRIS FARM

The Martin Harris farm is located on the west side of Maple Avenue approximately 1.5 miles north of the intersection of Church and Main Streets.

Historical Background

Martin Harris was born on 18 May 1783 at Easttown, Saratoga County, New York. His family moved to Palmyra in 1792. In 1794, Martin's father bought 600 acres in Palmyra for 50 cents an acre. Martin

Aerial Photograph, Palmyra, New York
(Martin Harris Farm — lower right)
Photograph courtesy of LDS Visual Resource Library — Craig W. Dimond, 1988

married Lucy Harris on 27 March 1808. He was baptized on 6 April 1830 at Fayette, New York.

Martin Harris financed the publication of the Book of Mormon and was one of the Three Witnesses. He served as a member of the Kirtland High Council and as a member of Zion's Camp and assisted in choosing twelve apostles in 1835.

Lucy Mack Smith described the events at the Harris farm in 1828 as follows:

> After leaving Joseph [in Harmony, Pennsylvania, Martin Harris] arrived at home with the manuscript in safety. Soon after he exhibited the manuscript to his wife and family. His wife was so pleased with it, that she gave him the privilege of locking it up in her own set of drawers, which was a special favor, for she had never before this allowed him even the privilege of looking into them . . . [Later,] previous to Joseph's arrival [in Palmyra,] Mr. Harris had been otherwise engaged, and thought but little about the manuscript. When Joseph sent for him, he went immediately to the drawer where he had left it, but, Behold it was gone! He asked his wife where it was. She solemnly averred that she did not know anything respecting it. He then made a faithful search throughout the house.[48]

CANAL PARK (ERIE CANAL)

The Canal Park is located just north of Highway 31, approximately a mile west of the intersection of Main and Church Streets.

Historical Background

The Erie Canal was a boon for farmers in New York who used it to ship their products to New York City. At Palmyra, the canal paralleled Mud Creek, near which Palmyra had been settled, and passed just a few hundred feet north of the village center at the corner of Main and Canandaigua. Since the first Erie Canal was dug, at least three different Erie canals have existed. The first, which the Saints used, is usually referred to as "Clinton's Ditch." It was forty feet wide and four feet deep and was completed at Palmyra in 1822.

The canal was enlarged in the 1840s and 1850s. It was eventually enlarged again and renamed the New York State Barge-Erie Canal. All three canals followed the same general route, so only bits and pieces of Clinton's Ditch are still visible.

The canal took missionaries to other regions in an effort to spread the news of the restoration; but before those early missions began, the canal brought individuals to the Smith home, where they found out about the "marvelous work and a wonder." Solomon Chamberlin related:

> I was then living on the Erie Canal forty miles below Rochester; I had occasion to go on a visit to Canada. I took boat for Lockport; when the boat came to Palmyra, I felt as if some *genie* or good spirit told me to leave the boat, and go or travel a south course; I did so for about three miles . . . [and] here my guide told me I must put up for the night; and I heard of the Smiths and the gold bible for the first time. I was now within half a mile of Joseph Smith's father's house where my guide had brought me. — In the morning the woman asked me if I had heard of the gold bible. I told her I had not; and there was something began on the top of my head and went to my toes like electricity; I said to myself I shall soon find why I have been led to this place in this singular manner . . . I soon arrived at the house and found Hyrum . . . Here I staid, and they instructed me in the manuscripts of the Book of Mormon; after I had been there two days, I went with Hyrum and some others to Palmyra printing office, where they began to print the Book of Mormon; and as soon as they had printed sixty-four pages I took them and started for Canada and preached to all.[49]

The Church was barely organized when Joseph Smith announced that the Lord had commanded his little flock to leave New York and "go to the Ohio."[50] Joseph himself left Fayette township for Kirtland, Ohio, sometime in January 1831. He asked the two hundred members of the Church to follow him as soon as they could.

The first group of Saints to leave New York for Ohio departed in early April 1831 under the direction of Newel Knight. They were from the Colesville area and followed the Old State Road north of Binghamton to Ithaca and then on boat up Cayuga Lake, then on the Cayuga and Seneca Canal for eleven miles, and then to Buffalo on the Erie Canal. The Erie Canal took them nearly 160 miles to Buffalo, where they took a steamer for 150 miles southwest to Fairport, Ohio, only eleven miles distance from Kirtland where the Saints were gathering.

Traveling by canal boat was less expensive and much more convenient and comfortable than overland travel in 1831. The cabins were usually divided into male and female quarters with bunk beds as many as four high for a reasonably comfortable sleep. The canal boats were pulled along by horses and by law were restricted to four miles per hour, or no more than ninety-four miles a day. The passengers usually stayed below in the main cabin or sat on the roof of the cabin. Passengers often jumped off the boat and walked along side to stretch their legs. Breakfast, lunch, and dinner were served each day. Local people had additional supplies and refreshments for sale along the canal route.

Eventually, two other organized Mormon groups left New York for Ohio. The Waterloo group (which was divided into two groups led by Lucy Mack Smith and Thomas B. Marsh) came from Fayette township; and the third group came from Palmyra and was led by Martin Harris. All three groups used the Erie Canal for their travel to Buffalo, New York.

Lucy Mack has left one of the few accounts of travel on the famous canal by the Saints. She wrote:

> We hired a boat of a certain Methodist preacher . . . When we were thus collected, we numbered eighty souls . . . Soon after this we were pushed off and under fine headway. I then called the brethren and sisters together, and reminded them that we were traveling by the commandment of the Lord, as much as father Lehi was, when he left Jerusalem . . . We then seated ourselves and sang a hymn . . . On getting about half way to Buffalo, the canal broke. This gave rise to much murmuring and discontentment . . . As the canal was repaired by eleven o'clock, we proceeded on our journey, and arrived at Buffalo on the fifth day after leaving Waterloo.[51]

Erie Canal near Palmyra, New York
(Lucy Mack Smith left New York using the Erie Canal)
Photograph courtesy of LDS Historical Dept. — Unknown, unknown

Fishers, New York

Fishers is located approximately twenty miles southwest of Palmyra, and two miles northeast of Mendon.

In 1792, the government established a fort at Fishers. It was part of a series of forts built along the frontier. On 11 November 1794, the Iroquois nation signed the Canandaigua Treaty; and the fort was abandoned (although it was used as a school and a church by the early settlers). One of the first settlers was John Fisher, Jr., after whom the village was named. His children built several mills, which enabled the area to grow.

In this area are several homes built by Brigham Young, including the Dutton–Woolston home on Main Street. The windows in the Fisher homestead, also on Main Street, were cut and glazed by Young in 1829.

PHINEAS HOWE YOUNG HOME

Phineas Young's home is located on the north side of Main Street at almost its west end.

Historical Background

Phineas Howe Young was born 16 February 1799 at Hopkinton, Middlesex, Massachusetts. He married Clarissa Hamilton on 18 January 1818. Young was baptized in April 1832.

Phineas Young records the details about his move to the Fisher-Mendon area as follows:

> In the fall of 1826, I became acquainted with Heber C. Kimball, in the town of Mendon, while on a visit there to see my brother-in-law, John P. Greene; and having understood that others of my father's family were going there, I concluded to sell out and move to Mendon, which I did in the spring of 1828. About this time my father, brother Lorenzo and others of my father's family, moved into the town. We immediately opened a house for preaching, and commenced teaching the people according to the light we had; a reformation commenced, and we soon had a good society organized, and the Lord blessed our labors. In April, 1830, having received the Book of Mormon, as I was on my way home from the town of Lima, where I had been to preach. . . . I bought the book and went home, and told my

Phineas Howe Young Home, Fishers, New York (Home has new siding)
(Early convert to Mormonism and brother to Brigham Young)
Photograph courtesy of the authors — Sheldon Fisher, 1988

wife I had got a week's work laid out, and I hoped that nothing would occur to prevent my accomplishing my task. She said, "Have you anything new to attend to?" I replied, "I have got a book here, called the Book of Mormon, and it is said to be a revelation, and I wish to read it and make myself acquainted with its errors, so that I can expose them to the world." I commenced and read every word in the book the same week. The week following I did the same, but to my surprise I could not find the errors I anticipated, but felt a conviction that the book was true.[52]

Mendon, New York

The Mendon township is located approximately eighteen miles southwest of Palmyra (twenty-two miles by road).

The first permanent settler in the Mendon area was Zebulon Norton in 1791. He decided to build a sawmill at Honeoye Falls. The township was divided into four hamlets — Mendon, Mendon Center, Sibleyville, and Rochester Junction. Mendon was organized on 26 May 1812. A number of neighborhoods were also in the township, including Tomlinson Corner, where the Youngs and Kimballs settled. Heber

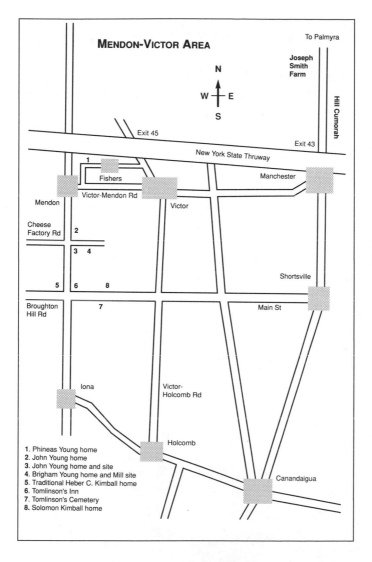

1. Phineas Young home
2. John Young home
3. John Young home and site
4. Brigham Young home and Mill site
5. Traditional Heber C. Kimball home
6. Tomlinson's Inn
7. Tomlinson's Cemetery
8. Solomon Kimball home

C. Kimball moved to the area in 1820 and became an apprentice potter at his brother's shop, a shop that Heber later purchased. The first member of the Young family to arrive in Mendon was John Young, Brigham's father. He arrived sometime in 1827 and bought eight acres of land from William Allen and, on 8 April 1830, forty acres from Marvin Burton. Brigham's date of arrival is less certain, but a local store record indicates that he was buying goods as early as 1828. While in Mendon, Brigham built a home and a shop on his father's property.

JOHN YOUNG HOME

The John Young farmhouse site is located on the southeast corner of the intersection of Highway 64 and Cheese Factory Road. On this site is part of the original farmhouse that was incorporated into the house still standing at this location. The major portion of the original John Young farmhouse is located across the street on the northeast corner of the intersection.

Historical Background

John Young was born on 7 March 1763 at Hopkinton, Middlesex County, Massachusetts. He married Abigail Howe in 1785 at Hopkinton, Massachusetts. Young was baptized on 5 April 1832 at Columbia, Pennsylvania. He moved to Kirtland, Ohio, in 1833, where he was ordained Patriarch.

Soon after John Young's arrival, several of his sons, including Brigham, moved to Mendon as well. Prior to this, Brigham had worked at a pail factory in Haydenville, New York; and he and his wife Miriam had lived in a home a few miles away in Port Byron. Brigham and his family lived with John for a short while until Brigham built his own home on the property soon thereafter.

John Young Farm, Mendon, New York
(Brigham Young's father's home)
Photograph courtesy of LDS Historical Dept. — Unknown, unknown

BRIGHAM YOUNG HOME SITE AND MILL POND

The Brigham Young home site is located just east of the John Young farmhouse site. The mill pond is located about three hundred yards southeast of the Brigham Young house site.

Historical Background

Miriam Works Young was born on approximately 6 June 1806 at Aurelius, Cayuga County, New York. She married Brigham Young on 8 October 1824 at Aurelius, New York. She was baptized in 1832 at Mendon, New York. She died on 8 September 1832 and was buried at Tomlinson Corner Cemetery in Mendon.

Sometime in 1832, Miriam contracted tuberculosis; and Brigham took over the duties of motherhood. He carried her to a rocking chair before leaving for work. Upon his return, he cooked dinner, cleaned up, read to Miriam, and then carried her back to bed. A neighbor later wrote,

Brigham Young Home, Port Byron, New York
(Identified as the Brigham and Miriam Young Home)
Photograph courtesy of LDS Historical Dept. — Unknown, unknown

Brigham Young Home Site and Mill Pond, Mendon, New York
(Early convert and leader of LDS Church)
Photograph courtesy of LDS Historical Dept. — Unknown, unknown

Mill Pond, Mendon, New York
(Site of early Church baptisms)
Photograph courtesy of LDS Historical Dept. — Unknown, unknown

There could scarcely be a more kind and affectionate husband and father than [Brigham] was, and few men in his circumstances would have provided better for their families. Mrs. Young was sick, most of the time unable to do any kind of work, but she was a worthy woman, and an exemplary Christian; she was well deserving of his care and attention.[53]

Heber C. Kimball was baptized by Elder Alpheus Gifford on 15 April 1832 in Trout Creek at the mill pond. As many as sixty individuals were baptized at this site. Thereafter, the mill pond was used only as a place to fish. Heber later reported,

I jumped up and pulled off my apron, washed my hands and started with him [Gifford] with my sleeves rolled up to my shoulders, and went the distance of one mile where he baptized me in a small stream in the woods. After I was baptized, I kneeled down and he laid his hands upon my head and confirmed me a member of the Church of Jesus Christ.[54]

Hayden Woolen Mills, Haydenville (Mentz), New York
(Earlier was a pail factory where Brigham Young worked)
Photograph taken from *Brigham Young, The New York Years* — Unknown, 1920

Heber C. Kimball Home, Mendon, New York
(Identified as Heber and Vilate Kimball's home)
Photo courtesy of LDS Historical Dept. — Unknown, unknown

TOMLINSON INN

Tomlinson Inn is located on the northeast corner of the intersection of Highway 64 and the Boughton Hill Road. The east part of the standing structure was the original inn.

Tomlinson Inn, Mendon, New York
(Early Mormon meeting place in the 1830s)
Photograph courtesy of LDS Historical Dept. — Unknown, unknown

Historical Background

Tomlinson Inn was a noted stagecoach hostelry with an attached dance hall. Phineas Young wrote,

> In April 1830 . . . I was on my way home from the town of Lima, where I had been to preach, I stopped at the house of a man by the name of Tomlinson, to get some dinner. While engaged in conversation with the family, a young man came in, and walking across the room to where I was sitting, held a book towards me, saying, — "There is a book, sir, I wish you to read." The thing appeared so novel to me that for a moment I hesitated, saying — "Pray sir, what book have you?" "The Book of Mormon, or, as it is called by some, the Golden Bible." "Ah, sir, then it purports to be a revelation." "Yes," said he, "it is a revelation from God." I took the book, and by his request looked at the testimony of the witnesses. Said he — "If you will read this book with a prayerful heart, and ask God to give you a witness, you will know the truth of this work." I told him I would do so, and then asked him his name. He said his name was Samuel H. Smith. "Ah," said I, "you are one of the witnesses." "Yes," said he, "I know the book to be a revelation from God, translated by the gift and power of the Holy Ghost, and that my brother Joseph Smith, jun., is a Prophet, Seer and Revelator."[55]

This book was instrumental in several conversions, including Brigham Young. Tomlinson, the inn owner, was also baptized; and the dance hall became the Mendon Branch meeting house for the Saints.

Heber C. Kimball recalled the situation at the branch during this period as follows:

> Women would come from Victor, a distance of three miles, to the town of Mendon, New York, where I lived: and I have seen them walk barefooted until they came near where I lived, and then they would put on their white stockings and shoes to go into meeting; and when they came out of meeting and had passed off a little out of sight, they would pull off their shoes and stockings and go home barefooted, for the purpose of saving their fine shoes and stockings they had spun and knit out of flax.[56]

TOMLINSON CORNER CEMETERY

Tomlinson Corner Cemetery is located approximately 0.3 mile east of Tomlinson Inn on Boughton Hill Road and is situated on the south side of the road.

Miriam Works Young Tombstone, Mendon, New York
(Tomlinson Corner Cemetery)
Photograph courtesy of LDS Historical Dept. — Unknown, unknown

Historical Background

Several members of the Young and Kimball families are buried here, including Heber C. Kimball's parents, his brother and sister-in-law (Charles and Judith Kimball), two of Heber C. and Vilate's children, Vilate's mother, and Miriam Works Young.

During Miriam Works Young's last stages of tuberculosis, Heber and Vilate Kimball brought her to their home where she died in September 1832. Brigham recalled,

> About three weeks afterwards (14 April 1832) my wife was also baptized. This was in the town of Mendon, in Monroe County. I tarried during the summer preaching the Gospel in the regions round about, baptizing and raising up churches. September 8th, 1832, my wife died of consumption, leaving me two little girls . . . In her expiring moments she clapped her hands and praised the Lord, and called upon brother Kimball and all around to praise the Lord. After my wife's death I made my home at bro. Kimball's.[57]

Miriam was buried in the Tomlinson Corner Cemetery a few days later. The present marker was placed there by her descendants. The Solomon F. Kimball marker states on one side, "Solomon F. Kimball Died July 9, 1825 Age 50 Father of Heber C. Kimball and Great-Grandfather of Spencer W. Kimball the 12th President of the Church of Jesus Christ of Latter-day Saints."

Solomon Kimball Home, Mendon, New York
(Identified as Heber C. Kimball's father's home)
Photograph courtesy of authors—T. Jeffery Cottle, 1990

SOLOMON KIMBALL HOME

The Solomon Kimball farm house is located approximately 0.7 mile east of Tomlinson's Inn on the north side of Boughton Hill Road.

Historical Background

Solomon Kimball was born in 1770 in Massachusetts. He married Anna Spaulding about 1794. Solomon died in Mendon on 9 July 1825.

Fayette, New York

The region that would eventually become Fayette originally belonged to the Cayuga Indians. In 1789, the Cayuga Nation ceded to

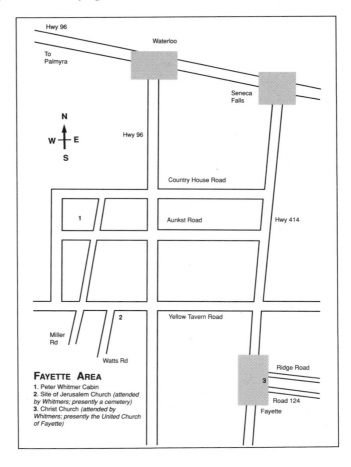

FAYETTE AREA
1. Peter Whitmer Cabin
2. Site of Jerusalem Church *(attended by Whitmers; presently a cemetery)*
3. Christ Church *(attended by Whitmers; presently the United Church of Fayette)*

the state of New York all of its lands, excluding the area of its reservation. The first settlers came to the area in 1789. The town of Fayette was initially named "Washington" on 14 March 1800. Its name was changed to Fayette on 6 April 1808. The town extended from the Seneca Lake to the Cayuga Lake. The township received its name from the Revolutionary War hero, General Gilbert Morier de La Fayette.

PETER WHITMER, SR. FARM

The Peter Whitmer, Sr. farm is approximately twenty-two miles from the Hill Cumorah. To get there from the Hill Cumorah, take the Canandaigua Road south to Manchester. From Manchester, take Highway 96 south to Waterloo and then to the Fayette area. The farm is situated about three miles south of Waterloo and about one mile west.

Another site of interest near the Whitmer farm is the Old Jerusalem Church site. Tradition indicates that several of the early Mormon services were held there. Seneca Lake, located approximately 3.5 miles from the Whitmer farm, was the site of many of the early baptisms.

Historical Background
Peter Whitmer, Sr. was born on 14 April 1773 in Pennsylvania. He married Mary Musselman sometime before 1798. Whitmer was

Peter Whitmer, Sr. Farm Site, Fayette, New York
(Smith finished Book of Mormon translation here in 1829)
Photograph courtesy of LDS Historical Dept. — George E. Anderson, 1908

baptized on 18 April 1830 by Oliver Cowdery in the Seneca Lake. Four of his sons were among the eight witnesses to the Book of Mormon, and another son was among the three witnesses.

Peter Whitmer's son brought Joseph Smith, along with Oliver Cowdery, from Pennsylvania to Peter Whitmer's home at Fayette. Here, Joseph completed the translation of the Book of Mormon. David Whitmer recalled an event that took place in his father's home in June 1829:

> One morning when [Joseph] was getting ready to continue the trans-
> lation, something went wrong about the house and he was put out
> about it. Something that Emma his wife, had done. Oliver and I
> went up stairs and Joseph came up soon after to continue the trans-
> lation, but he could not do anything. He could not translate a single
> syllable. He went down stairs, out into the orchard, and made sup-
> plication to the Lord; was gone about an hour—came back to the
> house, and asked Emma's forgiveness and then came up stairs where
> we were, and then the translation went on all right. He could do
> nothing save he was humble and faithful.[58]

During the process of translation, Joseph was informed that three individuals could see the plates besides himself. "Yea, and the testimony of three of my servants shall go forth with my words unto this generation," the Lord said to Joseph. "Yea, they shall know of a surety that these things are true, for I will give them power, that they may behold and view these things as they are, and to none else will I give this power to receive this same testimony among this generation."[59] This promise, given in Pennsylvania, was fulfilled in Fayette at the Whitmer farm. David Whitmer indicated that the following discussion occurred about 40 rods from his father's house:

> I was plowing in the field one morning and Joseph and Oliver came
> along with a revelation stating that I was to be one of the witnesses
> to the Book of Mormon. I got over the fence and we went out into
> the woods near by, and sat down on a log and talked awhile. We then
> kneeled down and Joseph prayed, We then got up and sat on the log
> and were talking, when all at once a light came down from above us
> and encircled us for quite a little distance around; and the angel stood
> before us. He was dressed in white, and spoke and called me by
> name and said "Blessed is he that keepeth His commandments." This
> is all that I heard the angel say. A table was set before us and on it
> the records were placed. The Records of the Nephites, from which
> the Book of Mormon was translated, the breast plates, the Ball of

Directors, the Sword of Laban and other plates. While we were viewing them the voice of God spoke out of heaven saying that the Book was true and the translation correct.[60]

The Whitmer farm was the site of many manifestations of God's power, including several important revelations.[61] Within a short time, though, the Saints received a revelation requiring them to move to Ohio. At the third conference of the Church, held on 2 January 1831 at the Whitmer home, Joseph received LDS D&C 38/RLDS D&C 38. Orson Pratt recalled:

> This brings to my mind a revelation which was given in a general conference on the 2d day of January 1831; the church then having been organized about nine months. All the Saints were gathered together from various little branches that had been established, in the house of old Father Whitmer, whose sons became conspicuous in this last dispensation as being witnesses of the Book of Mormon,— whose house also became conspicuous as the place where the Prophet Joseph Smith received many revelations and communications from

Peter Whitmer, Sr. Reconstructed Cabin, Fayette, New York
(Church of Christ organized here in 1830)
Photograph courtesy of LDS CES College Curriculum Dept.—Unknown, 1980

Seneca Lake, Fayette, New York
(Site of early Church baptisms in 1830s)
Photograph courtesy of the LDS Historical Dept. — George E. Anderson, 1907

heaven. In one small room of a log-house, nearly all the Latter-day Saints (East of Ohio) were collected together. They desired the Prophet of the Lord to inquire of God and receive a revelation to guide and instruct the Church that were then present. Brother Joseph seated himself at the table. Brother Sidney Rigdon, who was at the time a member of the Church, having just arrived from the West, where he embraced the Gospel through the administration of some of the Elders, was requested to act as scribe in writing the revelation from the mouth of the Prophet Joseph.[62]

Sometime after 5 January 1831, Joseph and Emma Smith left New York and moved to Ohio.

South Bainbridge (Afton), New York

South Bainbridge (Afton) is located approximately thirty miles northeast of Binghamton, a large city in southern New York.

The area of South Bainbridge (Afton) was settled by "Vermont Sufferers." They were settlers punished by the government of Vermont because of the civil disobedience and other actions they took when they did not want to be ruled by Vermont. Originally, this area was claimed by New Hampshire and New York. The dispute was settled by allowing Vermont to govern the area. Then, in 1786, New York Governor George Clinton bought the region. The first name of the area, "Clinton Township," was changed to "Jericho Township." In 1814, the Bainbridge Township was established.

SQUIRE TARBELL HOME SITE

The Squire Tarbell home site is located just north of Interstate 89. To get there, take the Highway 41 exit. The home site is west of Highway 41 between I-89 and the Susquehanna River. The site is on the present-day Afton Fairgrounds.

Historical Background

Squire Tarbell (Zachariah Tarbell or Tarble) was a lawyer and justice of the peace in South Bainbridge. He performed the marriage of Joseph and Emma at his home on 18 January 1827.

Squire Tarbell Home, South Bainbridge (Afton), New York
(Joseph and Emma Smith were married here in 1827)
Photograph courtesy of LDS CES College Curriculum Dept. — Unknown, unknown

Joseph Smith, Jr. met Emma Hale while in Pennsylvania working for Josiah Stowell in 1825. As he was preparing for a second visit to the area, young Joseph called his parents aside and said,

> "I have been very lonely ever since Alvin died, and I have concluded to get married; and if you have no objections to my uniting myself in marriage with Miss Emma Hale, she would be my choice in preference to any other woman I have ever seen." We were pleased with his choice, and not only consented to his marrying her, but requested him to bring her home with him, and live with us. Accordingly he set out with his father for Pennsylvania.[63]

Upon his arrival in Harmony, Joseph arranged Emma's visit at Stowell's residence. He asked her to marry him again. She had accepted the previous request, but her father refused to "give her hand" to Joseph. Emma accepted this second proposal on 18 January 1827 and was married by Tarbell at his home.

An official marker erected by the New York State Education Department in 1932 stands in front of the Afton Fairgrounds, the site of Squire Tarbell's home. It reads,

> MORMON HOUSE. Joseph Smith, founder of the Mormon Church was married in this house January 18, 1827 to Emily [Emma] Hale.

When the Colesville Branch of the Church left New York for Ohio in 1831, local Afton resident Harriet E. Shay recalled,

> I distinctly remember seeing the followers of Joseph Smith, Jr., of Mormon fame, go by my fathers, George Clappers, house on the east side of the Susquehanna River in the Town of Afton County of Chenango, N.Y. between Afton, formerly South Bainbridge, and Nineveh, on what is now known as the Lewis Poole farm. To the best of my recollection there were eight or ten wagons. They were covered like western emigrant wagons, and were drawn by oxen.[64]

Colesville, New York

Colesville is located approximated 10.5 miles southwest of South Bainbridge (Afton).

Colesville was permanently settled by John Lamphere in 1785. He brought his wife and two children from Connecticut to settle Colesville. The town was named for Nathaniel Cole, another early settler who arrived in the area in 1795.

Colesville is significant in the history of the Saints for several reasons. These include the facts that Emma Smith was baptized in Colesville and that it was the site of the first branch of the new church, the first miracle, and the first arrest of Joseph for his religious beliefs. An important and lifelong friend of Joseph Smith, Joseph Knight had a farm in Colesville. The Joseph Knight farm was located on the south side of the Susquehanna River, opposite the village of Nineveh and near the Colesville Bridge.

An account of the Knight property is contained in the following report:

> Just opposite of Nineveh, on the east side of the river, on what is now known as the Scott, or Henry P. Bush farm, in a little old, gray framed house lived a poor man named Knight who worked hard to sustain his little family. At the outlet of Pickerel Lake, on this farm, Knight had a carding mill, the dam trenches and raceways being still visible. In this mill Knight toiled from day to day to eke out the scanty supply for his little ones. Some distance west of the carding mill on a slight rise of ground, stands an old barn, in which Smith later preached to his disciples, giving forth his doctrines and revealing the new truth.[65]

Colesville, New York
(Early branch of Church established here at Joseph Knight's Farm)
Photograph courtesy of LDS Historical Dept. — George Anderson, 1907

Joseph Knight helped Joseph Smith during the first few years after the young prophet received the plates. Knight later wrote,

> Now he (Joseph) could not translate but little, being poor and nobody to write for him but his wife and she could not do much and take care of her house and he being poor and no means to live but work. His wife's father and family were all against him and would not help him. He and his wife came up to see me the first of the winter 1828 and told me his case. But I was not in easy circumstance and I did not know what it might amount to [me] and my wife and family [were] all against me about helping him. But I let him have some little provisions and some few things out of the store, a pair of shoes and three dollars in money to help him a little. In January his father and Samuel came from Manchester to my house when I was busy drawing lumber. I told him they had travailed far enough. I would go with my sleigh and take them down tomorrow. I went down and found them well and they were glad to see us. In the morning I gave the old man a half a dollar and Joseph a little money to buy paper to translate, I have but little with me.[66]

Later, when the Church began its move to Ohio, Knight put his farm up for sale. The following advertisement appeared in a local newspaper:

> FOR SALE, THE farm lately occupied by Joseph Knight, situated in the town of Colesville near the Colesville Bridge—bounded on one side by the Susquehanna River, and containing about one hundred and forty-two acres. On said Farm are two Dwelling Houses, a good Barn, and a fine Orchard. The terms of sale will be liberal—Apply to Wm. Waterman, Binghamton March 1, 1831[67]

PENNSYLVANIA

By 1609, Henry Hudson, an Englishman employed by the Dutch, had entered the Delaware Bay—thereby establishing Holland's claim to Pennsylvania. The first white settlers, however, were Swedes, in 1643. The first white to the interior of Pennsylvania was the Frenchman Etienne Brule, who explored the Susquehanna River to its source in 1615–16. The Swedes, who had established themselves on Tinicum Island near the Schuylkill River, ceded their claims to the Dutch in 1655; and eventually the English took possession of Dutch claims by 1664.

Charles II made William Penn proprietor of the lands west of the Delaware River in 1681. Before Penn arrived in the New World in October 1682, he had planned to create a new society for the Quakers, "A green Country Town, which will never be burnt and always be wholesome." Penn had his surveyor lay out the city of Philadelphia in the colony that bore his family name. The first white settlers built their community along the Delaware River and soon had eighty homes. By 1700, a Swedish pastor wrote, "If anyone were to see Philadelphia who had not been there before, he would be astonished beyond measure that it was founded less than twenty years ago."[1]

Pennsylvania began to industrialize early and was the host of the Continental Congress. This industrial advantage made Pennsylvania a pivotal colony during the Revolution. Valley Forge, Washington's Crossing, and Independence Hall are among the many national shrines in Pennsylvania. After the Revolution, the state was plagued by border disputes. Nevertheless, migration and settlements continued to grow. Among those who moved to the state was Isaac Hale.

Hale arrived in the northeastern section of Pennsylvania and settled near the Susquehanna River with his wife around 1791. Hale was originally from Connecticut but was raised in Vermont. He left Vermont seeking a better start for himself and his new wife. The area was already settled, but farm land was available. The Hales raised their family in the Harmony area and lived there the rest of their lives. Among their children was a daughter named Emma. Emma was born at Harmony in 1804 and lived with her father until she married Joseph Smith in 1827.

Mormon missionary activity in Pennsylvania began shortly after the Church of Christ was organized on 6 April 1830 at Fayette, New York. One of the first branches of the Church was organized at Columbia, Bradford County. Among the earliest missionaries to Pennsylvania were Orson Hyde, Samuel H. Smith, John F. Boynton, Evan Greene, Sidney Rigdon, and Erastus Snow.

Philadelphia, Pennsylvania

Philadelphia is located on the Delaware River across from the state of New Jersey.

Philadelphia was well situated for the capital city. It was located on the coast and within a short distance of several other major communities in the colonies. William Penn was granted this area in 1680. Penn reported, "I have led the greatest colony into America that ever man did upon a private credit."[2] Pennsylvania was the terminus of most of the trade routes and therefore made Philadelphia an important economic center during the early 1700s.

The farmers in the Great Valley of Virginia and the Carolinas found their best market in Philadelphia, and as a result, the city grew rapidly. During the pre-revolutionary period, Philadelphia remained an important educational and economic center. From the beginning of the American Revolution, Philadelphia symbolized the new political life in America.

After the organization of the LDS Church, missionaries spread the gospel to the major cities of the East, including Philadelphia. Soon thereafter, Joseph Smith and other Church leaders arrived in the city to conduct church business and to visit the Saints living in the area. Joseph Smith's history reports,

[21 December 1839] I arrived in Philadelphia, direct from Washington City, by the railroad, where I spent several days preaching and visiting from house to house, among the brethren and others.[3]

Joseph Smith had left Washington, D.C., after spending several frustrating days in the nation's capital trying to bring the Mormon question before the governmental leaders, including the President of the United States. Shortly after his arrival in the city of Philadelphia, he reported the following in his history:

[23 December 1839] About this time Brothers Rockwell and Higbee arrived at Philadelphia with my carriage from Washington, where they had been some time, leaving Elder Rigdon there sick, and Dr. Robert E. Foster to take care of him.[4]

Panoramic View, Philadelphia, Pennsylvania
(Joseph Smith, Jr. visited here in 1839-40)
Photo courtesy Historical Society of Pennsylvania — Frederick Langenheim, ca. 1840

While in the city, Joseph took the opportunity to visit members of the Church and to preach in various locations. On 30 December he left the city for a short visit:

[30 December 1839] About this time I left Philadelphia with Brother Orson Pratt, and visited a branch of the Church in Monmouth county, New Jersey, where I spent several days, and returned to Philadelphia.[5]

Joseph Smith's arrival in the city on 9 January 1840 preceded the arrival of Sidney Rigdon and Dr. Robert Foster on 14 January. While in Philadelphia, Joseph and other Church leaders visited members in and around the city. Finally, on 27 January 1840, Joseph left the city "in company with Brother Rockwell, Higbee, and Dr. Foster, traveling by railroad."[6]

The Church remained strong after Joseph's departure. The following fall, Orson Hyde presided at a church conference held in the city:

[17 October 1840] A conference was held in Philadelphia, Elder Orson Hyde presiding; 806 members were represented, including 24 Elders, 11 Priests, 6 Teachers, 5 Deacons, in Pennsylvania, New York City, New Jersey, and vicinity.[7]

The branch of the Church was flourishing, according to Parley P. Pratt when he called Benjamin Winchester to preside. A Church newspaper, *Gospel Reflector*, was published in the city beginning in 1841.

Along with Emma Hale, several other Mormons were born in Pennsylvania, including John Bernhisel, Jesse Gause, John Gaylord, Edward Hunter, Catherine Whitmer Page, Mary Brown Pulsipher, Sidney Rigdon, and David Whitmer.

Harmony, Pennsylvania

Harmony is located approximately three miles from the Pennsylvania and New York border and is situated about twenty-five miles southeast of Binghamton, New York.

In approximately 1786, Moses Comstock with his family came from Rhode Island to the Harmony area. At this time, the governors of New York and Pennsylvania were trying to determine the line between their states. A Pennsylvania resident, Colonel Timothy Picker-

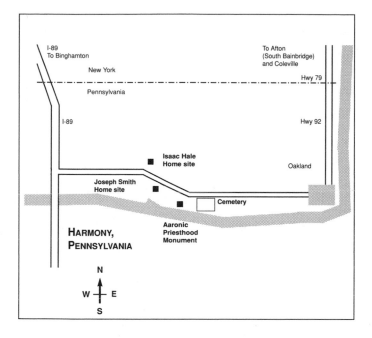

ing, had claimed the area. Several others were building roads and clear-ing and clearing land in an effort to develop the land. The actual state line between the states was not defined until 1793. As early as 1791, Issac Hale and Nathaniel Lewis lived near each other on the north side of the Susquehanna River. Harmony did not have a mill until 1820.

Joseph arrived in Harmony for the first time in November 1825. He and his father boarded in the Isaac Hale home during their brief employment with Josiah Stowell on a mining operation. Joseph later recorded, "during this time I was thus employed I was put to board with a Mr. Isaac Hale of that place (Harmony), Twas there that I first saw my wife, (his daughter) Emma Hale."[8]

The following account by David Hale (Isaac Hale's son) relates that after Isaac decided to go west, he explored the Harmony area and decided to settle there:

> After exploring the country, and getting acquainted with the oldest settlers, viz., Moses Comstock, Jonathan Bennett, Deacon Jedediah Adams, etc., he went back to Vermont, and married Elizabeth Lewis, Sister of Nathaniel Lewis, who married about the same time Sarah Cole, whose sister Lorana Cole, afterwards married Timothy Picker-ing, Jr. Well, now for the emigrant train, Isaac Hale And Nathaniel

Lewis, with their wives Elizabeth and Sarah. Nathaniel Lewis had a yoke of steers and a cart, on which to carry all their plunder [baggage], a distance of about two hundred and twenty miles from Wells, Rutland County, Vermont, to Willingborough, Lucerne County, Pennsylvania . . . [T]hey went through to Pennsylvania, as near as I can make it, in 1790. Isaac Hale bought an improvement of Jonathan Bennett. The land he afterward bought of Robert H. Rose, the same place on which I was raised, and on which he lived when I left my native place and where he was buried.[9]

Aerial Photograph, Harmony, Pennsylvania
(Harmony, modern Oakland and Hale farm site)
Photograph courtesy of USDA-ASGF Area Photography—Unknown, 1952

Emma's father was not entirely pleased with Joseph, with Joseph's occupation, or with Joseph's revelations. Isaac refused Joseph's marriage request for his daughter. Eventually, Joseph and Emma eloped and were married in New York. Initially, Isaac was greatly disturbed by the actions of his daughter and new son-in-law; nevertheless, he invited them back to Harmony after a short stay at the Smith home in Manchester.

Isaac Hale later recalled that soon after Joseph and Emma's return to Harmony, "I was informed they had brought a wonderful book of Plates down with them." Hale was shown the box; however, he was not allowed to look inside. "After this," he continued, " I became dissatisfied, and informed him that if there was anything in my house of that description, which I could not be allowed to see, he must take it away." [10]

Not long after this experience, Joseph and Emma purchased 13 1/2 acres from Isaac Hale and a small uncompleted home from Emma's brother, Jesse Hale. In the winter, Joseph and Emma moved the small two-room house to their newly acquired land about two hundred yards from the main home on Isaac's property. Both Joseph and Emma lived in this home during the next two and a half years. In August 1830, Joseph finally paid $200 for the land and home. On 12 April 1828, after Martin Harris' arrival from New York in February, the work of translation began. By 14 June, they had completed 116 pages of the translation.

After completion of the first 116 pages of translation, Joseph gave Martin the manuscript to take home with him to New York. The day after Harris' departure, Emma delivered her first son after a long and exhausting labor. The son was named after Joseph's brother, Alvin, and was born and died on the same day, 15 June 1828. Joseph and Emma buried the small infant in the cemetery near their home.

Eventually, Joseph made a short trip home to discover that the manuscript was lost. Joseph returned to Harmony and worked for a season farming and doing other jobs around the home. He met Oliver Cowdery near sunset on 5 April 1828 at Harmony. Oliver and Samuel Smith, Joseph's brother, arrived to meet the young prophet. While residing at the Smith home in Palmyra, Oliver had learned of Joseph's work. Joseph and Oliver talked late into the evening on that first Sunday night. Oliver decided to stay after Joseph told him his story.

On 7 April, two days following his arrival, Oliver Cowdery began acting as scribe to Joseph on the translation project. He later recorded,

"Day after day I continued, uninterrupted to write from his mouth, as he translated with the Urim and Thummim . . . [T]hese days were never to be forgotten, to sit under the sound of a voice dictated by the inspiration of heaven, awakened the utmost gratitude of this bosom."[11]

Despite two hard months of translation work and a meager diet, Joseph and Oliver enjoyed the unfolding of the Nephite story. Often, they paused to talk and to discuss what they had learned. During such a conversation, the question regarding baptism was discussed. "After writing the account given of the Savior's ministry to the remnant of the seed of Jacob upon this continent," Oliver wrote in 1834, "it was easy to be seen, that amid the great strife and noise concerning religion, none had authority from God to administer the ordinances of the gospel."[12]

They stopped the translation work and went from the home down to the river, a few hundred feet away. While praying to seek an answer to their question, Joseph and Oliver said that an angel appeared to them as in the brightness of day. The angel announced that he was the resurrected John the Baptist, the man who had baptized Jesus in the River Jordan. He worked under the direction of Peter, James, and John. "Upon you my fellow servants, in the name of Messiah I confer the Priesthood of Aaron, which holds the keys of the ministering of angels, and of the gospel of repentance, and of baptism by immersion for the remission of sins," the revelation continued.[13] Joseph and Oliver then went into the river where Joseph baptized Oliver and Oliver baptized Joseph. Then they ordained one another. The occasion was a joyous and happy one for both of them.

They had constant visitors from Palmyra during this period, including Joseph Smith, Sr. and Hyrum Smith.

Antagonism began to mount in Harmony during May of 1829. Early the next month, as a result of persecution that had become so intense that the work of translation stopped, David Whitmer arrived with his wagon and moved Joseph Smith and Oliver Cowdery to the home of David's father, Peter Whitmer, Sr., in Fayette, New York.

ISAAC HALE HOME SITE

The Isaac Hale home site is located approximately twenty-three miles from Binghamton, New York. To get there, proceed south on

Foundation of Isaac Hale Home, Harmony, Pennsylvania
(Emma Hale Smith's home before her marriage)
Photograph courtesy of Visual Resources Library — Craig W. Dimond, 1988

Interstate 89, take Highway 171, and travel approximately seven miles. The home site is situated on the north side of the highway.

Historical Background

Emma Hale Smith was born 10 July 1804 at Harmony, Susquehanna County, Pennsylvania. She married Joseph Smith, Jr. on 18 January 1827 at South Bainbridge, New York. She was baptized on 28 June 1830 at Colesville, New York. Emma was chosen the first president of the Nauvoo Female Relief Society on 17 March 1842.

After Joseph and Emma were married, they went to live with the Smiths in Manchester, New York. When Joseph and Emma returned to Harmony several weeks later, Isaac Hale said to his new son-in-law, with tear-filled eyes, "You have stolen my daughter and married her. I had much rather have followed her to her grave."[14]

The couple returned to New York where Joseph received the ancient record. Joseph said, "No sooner was it known that I had [the plates], than the most strenuous exertions were used to get them from me."[15] These problems, plus "intolerable" persecution of his family, led Joseph and Emma to move to her father's home in Harmony.

JOSEPH SMITH, JR. HOME SITE

The Joseph Smith, Jr. home site is located on the south side of Highway 171 just southeast of the Issac Hale home site.

Historical Background

Just off the northeast corner of the old foundation site, the LDS Church has placed a marker that states,

NEAR THIS PLACE in the village of Harmony, Pennsylvania, much of the Book of Mormon was translated by the modern American Prophet Joseph Smith. His wife, Emma Hale Smith, was a native of Harmony. Her parents, Mr. and Mrs. Isaac Hale invited Joseph and Emma to come to Harmony from Manchester, Ontario County, New York, where they lived in 1827. In the Hale home, Joseph worked on the translation of the sacred record which told the history of the ancient inhabitants of America. This record, engraved on plates of gold, had been given to Joseph Smith by Moroni, who came to him as a heavenly messenger. Moroni, while living on the earth as a mortal being, was the last of a great people who inhabited ancient America, but was destroyed in war about 420 A.D. He hid the record in the earth for safekeeping. Under the direction of God, Moroni

Joseph and Emma Smith Home, Harmony, Pennsylvania
(Joseph and Emma lived here between 1827 and 1830)
Photograph courtesy of LDS Historical Dept. — Unknown, unknown

returned to the earth in 1827 and placed the record in the custody of Joseph Smith as part of a modern restoration of the gospel of the Lord Jesus Christ. Though unschooled, Joseph translated it by divine power and published it as The Book of Mormon in Palmyra, New York, in 1829 [1830].

PRIESTHOOD RESTORATION MONUMENT

The Priesthood Restoration Monument is located approximately one hundred yards southeast of the Joseph Smith, Jr. home site.

Historical Background

In 1834, in the Church's newspaper published at Kirtland, Oliver Cowdery published an account of the Aaronic Priesthood restoration. An abstract from this account stated,

> After writing the account given of the Savior's ministry to the remnant of the seed of Jacob, upon this continent, it was easy to be seen . . . that amid the great strife and noise concerning religion, none had authority from God to administer the ordinances of the gospel. For, the question might be asked, have men authority to administer

Joseph and Emma Smith Home, Harmony, Pennsylvania
(Book of Mormon translation occurred here)
Photograph courtesy of Utah State Historical Society — Unknown, unknown

in the name of Christ, who deny revelations? . . . Our souls were driven out in mighty prayer to know how we might obtain the blessings of baptism and of the Holy Spirit, according to the order of God, and we diligently sought for the right of the fathers, and the authority of the holy priesthood . . . On a sudden, as from the midst of eternity, the voice of the Redeemer spake peace to us, while the veil was parted and the angel of God came down clothed in glory, and delivered the anxiously looked for message, and the keys of the gospel of repentance! What joy! what wonder! what amazement! . . . our eyes behold — our ears heard. As in the "blaze of day"; yes, more — above the glitter of the May sun beam, which then shed its brilliancy over the face of nature! Then his voice, though mild, pierced to the center, and his words, "I am thy fellow servant," dispelled every fear. We listened — we gazed — we admired! 'Twas the voice of the angel of glory — 'twas a message from the Most High! and as we heard we rejoiced . . . What joy filled our hearts and with what surprise we must have bowed . . . when we received under his hand the holy priesthood, . . . [We] were ordained by the angel John unto the lesser or Aaronic priesthood . . . [A]s he said, "Upon you my fellow servants, in the name of Messiah I confer this priesthood and this authority, which shall remain upon the earth, that the sons of Levi may yet offer an offering unto the Lord in righteousness!"[16]

Susquehanna River, Harmony, Pennsylvania
(Priesthood restored near here in 1829)
Photograph courtesy of LDS Historical Dept. — Unknown, unknown

MCKUNE CEMETERY

The McKune Cemetery is located approximately one hundred yards east of the Priesthood Restoration Monument.

Historical Background

Joseph and Emma buried their first-born son, Alvin, in the McKune Cemetery after his death on 15 June 1828. Emma's parents, Isaac and Elizabeth Hale, are also buried there. Isaac Hale's tombstone reads,

ISAAC HALE died Jan. 11, 1839, age 75 yrs. 10 mo. & 10 ds. The body of Isaac Hale, the Hunter, like the cover of an old book, its contents torn out, and stripped of its lettering and gilding, lies here food for worms, yet the work itself shall not be lost for it will as he believed: appear once more in a new and more beautiful edition, corrected and amended.

Isaac and Elizabeth Hale Tombstones, Harmony, Pennsylvania
(Emma Hale Smith's parents)
Photograph courtesy of LDS Historical Dept. — George E. Anderson, 1907

Alvin Smith Tombstone, Harmony, Pennsylvania
(First child of Joseph and Emma Smith, died in 1828)
Photograph courtesy of LDS Historical Dept. — George E. Anderson, 1907

An official New York State marker stands near the road at the cemetery and reads,

> JOSEPH SMITH. The founder of Mormonism lived in this vicinity about 1825-29. His infant son is buried in the cemetery. Much of the translation of the "Golden Plates" for the Book of Mormon was done nearby.

OLD SPANISH MINE SITE

The old Spanish mine site is located approximately twenty-five miles south of Colesville near Harmony, Pennsylvania.

After the economic setback in New England, the Smith family continually engaged in efforts to support themselves, often engaging in employment off the farm. For the oldest children, this situation often meant living and working for someone else. Josiah Stowell hired Joseph Smith on several occasions, paying him $14 a month plus room and board to work at Josiah's mill or on his farm. The property was on the Susquehanna River near South Bainbridge. During this same period,

Money Hole, Harmony, Pennsylvania
(Identified as old Spanish mine)
Photograph courtesy of LDS Historical Dept. — George E, Anderson, 1907

Joseph worked for Joseph Knight when not employed by Stowell. Knight's property was on the south (or east) side of the river, three and a half miles downstream from Stowell's farm and just a few miles north of the Pennsylvania border.

Josiah Stowell believed he had located an old Spanish mine in the area, about twenty-five miles south near Harmony, Pennsylvania. During the summer of 1825, Stowell had put hired hands to work to locate the mine — but without success. Consequently, Stowell, who had heard that young Joseph Smith of Palmyra had the gift to find hidden objects, hired Father Smith and his son. Young Joseph agreed to help find the lost Spanish mine in 1825, when the family needed money. Joseph was under pressure from his father and eager friends to assist Stowell in his search for buried treasure, the kind of work he did not like. Besides the pressure from family and friends, cruel and unrelenting poverty was a constant reality to young Joseph and was an added pressure. Eventually, Joseph dissuaded Stowell from the adventure, but Joseph's employment with Stowell plagued him during his life as Joseph attempted to restore the Church of Christ.

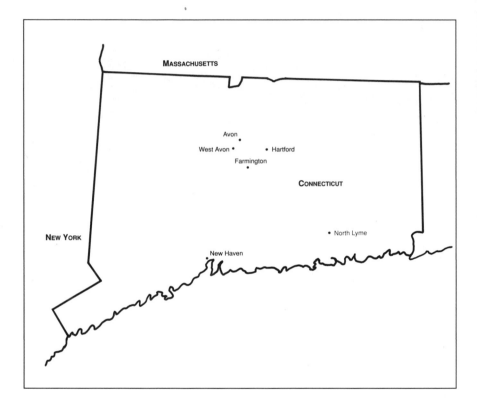

CONNECTICUT

The native American Indians called the Connecticut River "Quinnehtuqut," the long tidal river. The first white settlers established their villages on this river. A trading post was established at Windsor in 1633, and other settlements followed soon thereafter. English settlement began when Reverend Thomas Hooker fled Massachusetts Bay Colony because of the oppressive Puritan laws and established Hartford on the site of a former Dutch trading post in 1646.

Joseph Smith's maternal grandfather, Solomon Mack, was born in Lyme, Connecticut, in 1732. Financial difficulties broke up the Mack family. Young Solomon was "bound out" as a laborer to a neighbor. On obtaining his release from service, Solomon enlisted in the army and fought in the French and Indian War. In 1759, he married Lydia Gates, the daughter of a prominent Connecticut deacon.

Over the years Solomon had a large amount of land in Lyme, but he closed out these holdings between 1762 and 1766, disposing of 127 acres with house and farm building. The Macks then moved some one hundred and thirty miles north to New Hampshire in 1761.

The Industrial Revolution began at about the same time as the American Revolution, and paper mills appeared at Norwich and near Hartford beginning in 1768. In 1788, the first woolen mills began operation in Hartford. Wilford Woodruff's family operated sawmills and lived at Farmington (Avon), near Hartford, for three generations. He and several members of his family would be converted by Mormon missionaries in the 1830s. Elder Orson Hyde and Samuel H. Smith are reported to have been the first missionaries in Connecticut, arriving there in 1832. Others followed them, including Wilford Woodruff.

Various branches of the Church were organized throughout the state, including Hartford and New Haven.

"Aunt" Jane James, a black born at Wilton, Fairfield County, Connecticut, on 11 May 1821, was an early convert of the LDS Church in Connecticut. While a young girl there, she lived as a servant, not a slave, in the home of a prosperous white family. Jane James was a Presbyterian when Charles Wandell, a Mormon missionary, arrived in the area with his companion. Eventually, she was converted by the message and introduced her own family to the Church. Soon thereafter, Jane and eight family members emigrated to the Church headquarters in Illinois, where she met Joseph Smith.

Jane James recalled that when she met Joseph Smith in Nauvoo for the first time,

> I was certain he was a prophet because I knew it. I was willing to come and gather, and when he came in with Dr. Bernhisel I knew him. Did not have to tell me because I knew him. I knew him when I saw him in old Connecticut in a vision, saw him plain and knew he was a prophet.[1]

Several other well-known Mormons born in Connecticut were John S. Carter, Simeon Carter, Salmon Gee, Joseph Kingsbury, Orson Hyde, Orson Pratt, Aurelia S. Rogers, Jerusha Barden Smith, Elizabeth Ann Whitney, F. G. Williams and Wilford Woodruff.

Avon, Connecticut

Avon is located approximately eight miles west and slightly north of Hartford, Connecticut.

Located north of Farmington, Avon was settled in approximately 1666. Three families, the Harts, Norths, and Woodforths, were the core families of these early settlers. Many intermarriages occurred among these families, and the community grew as the children of these early settlers built homes near their parents.

By 1749, thirty-one families were residents of Avon. By 1750, they had their own church organization, which met in the different homes. However, not until June 1830 was the town of Avon actually incorporated. Eldad Woodruff apparently settled in Avon (Farmington area) in 1706. At this time, he acquired the sawmill, gristmill, and

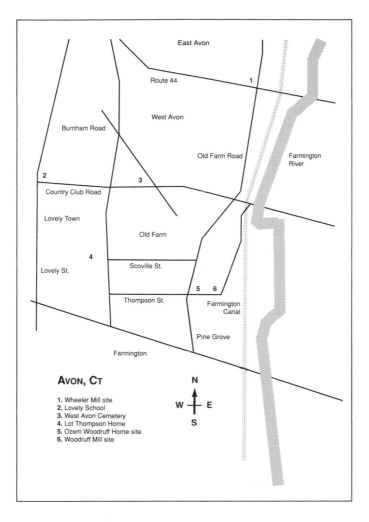

AVON, CT

1. Wheeler Mill site
2. Lovely School
3. West Avon Cemetery
4. Lot Thompson Home
5. Ozem Woodruff Home site
6. Woodruff Mill site

carding machine. Wilford Woodruff worked in the family mills until he moved to Richland, New York, in 1832.

Both Wilford Woodruff's father and grandfather were born in Farmington. Woodruff, like his father, worked in the mills. Woodruff wrote, "I assisted my father in the Farmington mills until I was twenty years of age."[2]

Woodruff eventually left the Farmington area and settled in Richland, New York, where he was baptized on 13 December 1833. He gathered with the Saints in Ohio, where he married Phoebe Carter in Kirtland. In July 1837, Woodruff returned to his ancestral home on

Avon, Connecticut
(Birthplace of Wilford Woodruff in 1801)
Photograph courtesy of Avon Historical Society — Unknown, ca. 1890

a missionary journey. He arrived in Avon on 5 July 1837 and wrote the following in his journal:

> Spent the night at Aunt Helen Wheelers. Visited my kinsman and former friends in the place . . . July 6th A view of the place of my nativity. This was a day of great interest to me. I left Aunt Wheelers, after visiting Daniel Luther, and many in the place. I was in company with Elder Hale on the canal to Uncle Adna Hart's. From thence to Woodfords' mills built and formerly owned by my father Aphek Woodruff. I was born and spent my youth upon the place. After viewing the mills, I walked to the house where I was born and visited each apartment. The house and farm all looked natural, Bougue Hill not accepted. I called at Mr. Henry Woodford's and saw Mrs. Woodford. I also called upon Mr. Judds., Mrs. Allens, Z. and O. Harts, at Roger Woodfords I saw Eldad W. and Lavilla Day.[3]

A happy experience was a visit to his father's home:

> After spending most of the day in visiting the before mentioned friends I walked from Ozem Woodruff's to Farmington to again visit my Parents who had moved from Colebrook, a few days previous, to their former place of residence. I arrived at my father's house at the setting of the sun where I was once more in life blessed with the

Eldad Woodruff Home, Farmington, Connecticut
(Wilford Woodruff's grandfather's home)
Photograph from *Contributor* Vol. 13 (September 1892) —Junius F. Wells, ca. 1892

happy privilege of taking my parents by the hand and of beholding
them face to face after being separated from them rising of five years.
I was joyfully received and made heartily welcome. I visited the mills
where I had spent several years and found things looked natural I
spent the night pleasantly at my father's house. Distance of the day
16 miles.[4]

His journal is full of expressions of appreciation for the kindness
that was shown him, but he also records many memories of his childhood. Nevertheless, his mission to Connecticut was more than a family
reunion. It was an opportunity for Wilford to share the Book of Mormon with his family and friends.

During one afternoon, Wilford visited a pine grove where he often
went to meditate as a young man. "I visited a pine grove," he wrote,
"that I often retired to in 1830 for prayer and meditation. I had many
interesting seasons by day and by night while tending a mill for Collins
in 1830, in the pine grove above spoken of. I spent 3 hours in this
grove reading the Book of Mormon and [in] prayer."[5]

Aphek Woodruff Home, Avon, Connecticut
(Wilford Woodruff's father's home)
Photograph from *Contributor* Vol. 13 (September 1892) —Junius F. Wells, ca. 1892

WEST AVON CEMETERY

The West Avon Cemetery is located on the northwest corner of Country Club Road and Burmham Road.

Historical Background

Several generations of Woodruff ancestors were buried at this cemetery, including his mother and grandparents. During his visit to Avon in 1837, Woodruff went to the local cemetery and visited the graves of his ancestors. Of this occasion, he said:

> I gazed upon it and also upon the grave yard in which lay the bones of many of my progenitors and friends my mother not accepted. In visiting their tombs I read the inscription of several numbered with the dead who were well when I left Connecticut in 1832. I read the following inscription upon the tomb stone of my Mother BULAH WOODRUFF the daughter of Lot Thompson: A pleasing form a generous gentle heart a good companion just without art Just in her dealings faithful to her friend Beloved through life lamented in the

Eldad and Dinah Woodruffs' Tombstones, Avon, Connecticut
(Wilford Woodruff's grandparents' tombstones)
Photograph from *Contributor* Vol. 13 (September 1892) —Junius F. Wells, ca. 1892

end. Bulah Thompson Woodruff was born 1782 Died June 11th 1808 Aged 26 years.[6]

The tombstones of his grandfather and grandmother have the following inscriptions:

In memory of Lieut. Eldad Woodruff, who departed this life Dec. 28th, 1805, in the 58th year of his age. Pity the weeping widow's woe. And be her counselor and stay. Adopt the fatherless and smooth to useful happy life their way.

In memory of Widow Dinah, wife of Eldad Woodruff who died June 12, 1822 [Age] 72.

WHEELER MILL SITE

The Wheeler mill site is located at the corner of Route 44 and Old Farms Road.

Wheeler Mill, Avon, Connecticut
(Woodruff worked here as a young man)
Photograph courtesy of Avon Historical Society — Frank Hadsell, ca. 1900

Historical Background

As a young man, Wilford worked for his Aunt Wheeler at this mill. He recalled one of the many accidents he encountered growing up in Avon (Farmington):

> In 1827 while managing a flour mill for Aunt Wheeler, in Avon, Conn., I was standing upon one of the Wheels, clearing away the ice. A man, not knowing I was in that position, hoisted the gate and turned upon the wheel a full head of water. The wheel started at once, my foot slipped, and I was plunged head foremost over the rim of the wheel into about three feet of water, my weight had drawn my legs out of the wheel or I would have been drug under a shaft and crushed to death.[7]

LOVELY SCHOOLHOUSE

The Lovely Schoolhouse is located on the northwest corner of Lovely Street and Country Club Road.

Historical Background

Woodruff preached a number of sermons while in Avon and in the surrounding communities. While in Avon, he preached at the Lovely Schoolhouse during his first visit in 1837 and again upon a return visit in 1838.

> [10 July 1837] I preached at the Lovely Street Schoolhouse to a full congregation of relatives and friends that gave strict attention and treated me with kindness. The Spirit of God rested upon us.[8]

> [11 July 1837] I preached at the Lovely Street Schoolhouse at candle light upon the authenticity of the Book of Mormon. The people gave good attention. I spent the night at uncle Ozem Woodruff's. We conversed upon the things of the Kingdom until the following day.[9]

> [24 June 1838] Sunday I called upon William Cowles to see a sick child of Brother Ozem Woodruff. I preached in the Lovely Street Schoolhouse in the forenoon. I preached upon the reign of Christ from Job 19, 23 to 28. I also preached in the afternoon at the same place it being the last time I ever preached to my friends in that place.[10]

Lovely Street School, Avon, Connecticut
(Wilford Woodruff preached here in 1837-38)
Photograph courtesy of Avon Historical Society — Unknown, before 1898

WOODRUFF FAMILY MILL SITE

The Woodruff family mill site is located on Thompson Road where the Avon Old Farm School is now located.

Historical Background

While a child, Woodruff experienced several accidents, including one at his father's mill. He recorded,

> My father owned a saw mill in addition to his flour mill, and one morning, in company with several other boys, I went into the saw mill and got upon the headlock of the carriage to ride, not anticipating any danger; but before I was aware of it my leg was caught between the headlock and the fender post and broken in two. I was taken to the house, and lay nine hours before my bones were replaced. That time was spent in severe pain; but being young, my bones soon knitted together, and in a few weeks I was upon my feet as usual, attending to the sports of youth.[11]

Woodruff Family Mill, Avon, Connecticut
(Woodruff worked here as a young man)
Photograph courtesy of Avon Historical Society—Unknown, ca. 1890

OZEM WOODRUFF HOME SITE

The Ozem Woodruff home site is located near the Woodruff family mill site on Thompson Road where the Avon Old Farm School is now located.

Historical Background

Just a few days after his arrival in Avon, Wilford visited the home of his Uncle Ozem. He wrote of this first visit,

> [I] walked to Uncle Ozem Woodruff and found him at home. I was truly rejoiced to once more take this dear friend by the hand. Oft hath this friend led me by the hand in my youth. Oft hath uncle Ozem taught me the gifts and graces of the Church of Christ. I saw him in the celestial kingdom in a vision. Oh God, have mercy upon him and enable him to stand in the new and everlasting covenant.[12]

Wilford's prayer was answered several days later when on the 12th, he recorded,

> During the night at 2 o'clock a.m. Uncle Ozem Woodruff and his household believed the fullness of the everlasting gospel and I led

Ozem Woodruff Home, Avon, Connecticut
(Woodruff's uncle's home)
Photograph from *Contributor* Vol. 13 (September 1892) —Junius F. Wells, ca. 1892

them forth at the same hour of the night and baptized them for the remission of their sins, being three of them, viz. Ozem Woodruff, Hannah Woodruff, and John Woodruff, their son. Glory to God in the Highest for this blessing. The Lord hath given me the desires of my heart in this thing which is in fulfillment of a vision given me in 1818. All is now fulfilled.[13]

LOT THOMPSON HOME

The Lot Thompson Home is located on West Avon Road near Scoville Street.

Historical Background

Wilford Woodruff's mother was born here; and, after her death, Wilford spent time with his grandparents. Upon his arrival in Avon in 1837, Wilford visited his relatives in this home several times.

> I walked from my father's house into the west street of Avon. I called upon uncle Thadeus Thompson, Grandmother Thompson and her

Lot Thompson Home, Avon, Connecticut
(Birthplace of Wilford Woodruff's mother)
Photograph from *Contributor* Vol. 13 (September 1892) —Junius F. Wells, ca. 1892

household and many other relatives and neighbors all of which manifested pleasure in seeing me.[14]

For Wilford, this trip to Connecticut was a time to reflect on his
early childhood and to share with his friends and family the "everlast-
ing gospel" which meant so much to him.

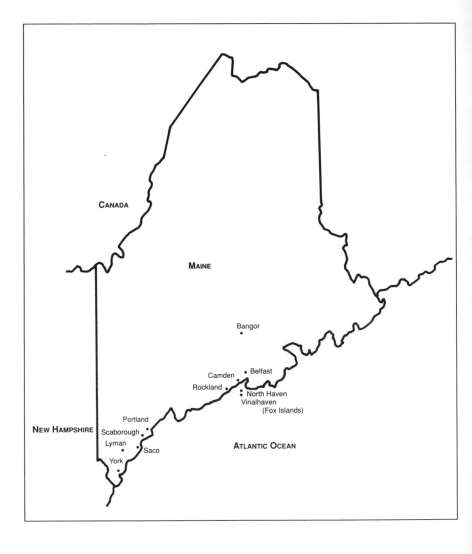

MAINE

The first Europeans to visit Maine may have been the Norsemen around A.D. 1000. John Cabot, Givovanni da Verrazano, and Esteban Gomez visited the coast of Maine during the sixteenth century. Algonquin Indian tribes lived in the area when John Smith's 1614 expedition explored, mapped, and named the area "New England."

The first white settlement established in 1607 was at the mouth of the Kennebec River, Popham. Within a year, the settlement was abandoned, but not before the first vessel built in America (the *Virginia*) was completed there. The first permanent settlement was York, founded in 1624. Other settlements followed in the early 1630s.

Massachusetts assumed judicial control over Maine in 1652, and in 1677 the original patent was sold to Massachusetts. In 1641, the English crown chartered York as the first city in America. This charter, however, did not end French interests and claims to the area.

The French, allied with local Indian tribes, fought for their claims. From the 1670s to the end of the "Queen Anne's War" in 1713, southern Maine was racked by a series of brutal battles and attacks by both whites and Indians.

While French influence came to an end in 1759 at the conclusion of the French and Indian War, the formal surrender of interests occurred at the signing of the Treaty of Paris in 1763.

Except for the British raid on Farmouth, southern Maine witnessed no fighting during the Revolution. A primitive road ran parallel to the coast up to the Kennebec River from Kittery at the border between New Hampshire and Maine. The interior was settled a distance of only about twenty miles from the shore, with some deep settlement along the major rivers in the area.

Mormon missionaries arrived in Maine from New Hampshire and Massachusetts shortly after the organization of the Church in New York in 1830. Many of these missionaries came to Maine with referrals from family members and friends who had converted to Mormonism elsewhere and now wanted their friends and family to hear the message of the restoration.

Among the early converts in Maine was Patty B. Sessions. Patty was born at Bethel, Maine, in 1795. She married David Sessions on 28 June 1812 and settled on a farm at Ketcham, Maine. Patty was baptized into the Methodist faith four years later in 1816; her husband soon followed her. The family remained active in the Methodist Church until their conversion to Mormonism in 1834. One year following her baptism, Patty attended an LDS Church conference where Mormon Apostle Brigham Young presided. "The gathering of the Saints was taught," she recalled, "and preparations began to be made to remove to Zion."[1] On 5 June 1837, the Sessions family began their journey to Missouri, leaving lifelong friends and family in Maine. Other Mormon converts from Maine followed the Sessions west as missionary work spread throughout the area during the first decades of the infant church's existence.

Other branches established in Maine remained in communication with Church leaders through missionary contacts, church conferences, and church periodicals such as the *Messenger and Advocate*, published in Ohio.

The Church newspaper often printed information and news about various Church branches in the East. From Maine, the *Messenger and Advocate* announced the death of a faithful Latter-day Saint, William Andrews:

> In Hollis, Maine, Sept. 3rd. brother WILLIAM ANDREWS, aged 82 years. Our aged brother was a soldier of the Revolution; served 2 years at one time, and was appointed to guard Gen. Washington's Baggage Wagons from Mass. to the South. At the close of the War he received an honorable and regular discharge; and several years has drawn a pension. After the peace of 1782, he purchased a situation at Buxton, County of York, (district) now State of Maine, on which he resided till his death . . . In the summer of 1833 he was received into the Church of the Latter Day Saints and has continued till his death to adorn his profession.[2]

Maine has a rich LDS Church history and was the birthplace of several Latter-day Saints, including Sam Brannon, Josiah Butterfield, Jesse C. Little, and Phoebe Carter Woodruff.

York, Maine

York is located just north of the Maine and New Hampshire border and is situated on the coast.

The first white permanent settlement in York occurred in the early 1600s. In 1639, the territory was given by a British royal charter to Sir Ferdinando Gorges. The village was first named Gorgeana but in 1652 was reorganized as a town and renamed York. In 1832, the first Mormon missionaries arrived at the settlements in York County. Before their arrival, however, the first anti–Mormon article appeared in Maine in the fall of 1831. The *Christian Mirror*, published in Portland, carried extracts from the Ezra Booth letters on 24 November 1831.

The first missionaries in New England traveled over two thousand miles from Church headquarters in Kirtland, Ohio, through New England and back to Ohio. Orson Hyde and Samuel Smith left Kirtland in the spring of 1832, in fulfillment of a mission call received on 25 January 1832 at a Church conference in Amherst, Ohio.[3]

Orson Hyde described his travel through Maine in his missionary journal:

> 19th [October] went from house to house on the back roads [Portsmouth, New Hampshire area] until noon and warned the people and then came on the main road and crossed the Piscataqua River in a canoe one mile wide, and then we were in the State of Maine went from House to House, but not much progress this day tarried all night with a man that was rather inebriated with liquor, he dreamed that he plead with us for a Book until we let him have one and he dreamed the same things three times and in the morning he pleaded so hard we left one and he promised to lend it to others etc.[4]

Although the work was difficult, a branch of the Church was eventually organized in York County. Hyde stated,

> Went from house to house found some friendly and others hard. Tarried all night with a man there who was a Methodist minister and his wife put [us] up and in the morning had some conversation with him and wrote down some ideas respecting the Book of Mormon

Town Center, York, Maine
(Orson Hyde and Samuel Smith visited here in 1832)
Photograph courtesy of Old York Historical and Improvement Society — Unknown,
    about 1868

and the fulness of the scriptures many quotations from the scriptures
and we tried to get the Methodist meeting house to preach but the
priest set up in opposition to it and we did not get it and we went
on.[5]

On the 21st of October, Hyde and Smith went to York township:

Went to York house to house but I could not get faith for the people
to bring them to the work. Prayed with a number of families but
could not get much faith for them. Well has the Lord said, they will
not repent, tarried all night with W. Langley where we got some
washing done etc. he was a professor of religion but seemed to be
friendly. 22 [October] tarried during the day with M. W. Langley,
studied some etc held meeting in the evening at his house quite a
number came out and we preached to them, tarried all night at his
house could not get him to realize the importance of gathering out
from the wicked.[6]

Eventually, another request came for a "preaching appointment"; and on 23 October, Hyde and Smith went to a nearby school house some two miles from Langley's home. At the school house, about forty to fifty people attended a morning meeting; and Hyde believed that the meeting was very successful. In the afternoon, he wrote,

> There came out a house full, had great liberty in speaking upon the gathering and the second coming of Christ spake with authority the Lord was with me. [I] gave them [the congregation] a call to arise [and be] baptized and go forth, many I saw were cut down and melted into tears which gave us some hope, never saw better attention paid.[7]

Hyde and Smith approached York Village on 24 October. On the way, they "stopped [at] a house to get some new cider they asked us to take dinner with them, and there was a Young, [a] methodist minister came in and we had some conversation" which, according to Hyde, the minister "made light of." Hyde responded that it "was a serious matter . . . [H]e felt considerably reproved." After their departure, the missionaries were "overtaken by the minister and talked with him a

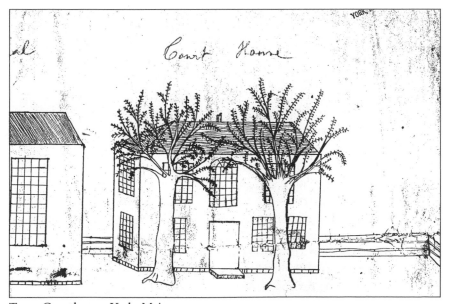

Town Courthouse, York, Maine
(Missionaries preached here in 1832)
Drawing courtesy of Old York Historical and Improvement Society — Unknown, unknown

mile or two, and then stopped in the road and talked and read about an hour and he was anxious to buy one of the Books." Because they had only two copies between themselves, they were unable to make a copy available for his use. "[H]e seemed to be quite anxious," Hyde recounted, and "could not shake it off." An invitation was given to visit his home, which the missionaries gladly accepted. In York Village, they stayed at the Young home.[8]

The following day, the missionaries "gave out the appointment." Samuel Smith noted, "[We] obtained liberty to preach in the court house for we went into the village and we put up a notice upon a board fence."[9] Their work continued as they went from house to house until the evening before the scheduled meeting at the court house. They arrived at the meeting and found a large number of people in attendance. It was a great meeting. Hyde wrote:

> I had great liberty more so than I had before, and I thought of what Joseph said, "I should lift up my voice like an angel of God" the people arose all and retired in almost perfect silence one man asked us where we were going to stay I told him we did not know and he told us to go in to the tavern and some of them would come shortly, two come in and one said if we tarried at the tavern he would pay the bill and the other said if we would go home with him we should be welcomed, we thanked them for their kindness and went home with the man.[10]

Smith's journal agrees with Hyde's sentiments about the meeting: "[A]t night a large congregation came together and Brother Orson preached to them and he was strengthened much by the Spirit of the Lord and I have testimony to many things that had been said."[11] On 26 October, the missionaries left York Village for Wells, which was a little north but still in York County.

Eventually, their labors in the county yielded success. Near Saco, the missionaries baptized a young man, Timothy Smith. Samuel Smith recorded, "helped dig potatoes a bit while there a young man came by the name of Timothy Smith. He had heard us preach and was convinced of the truth of the things we said."[12] While there, a young girl died of consumption. The family asked the young missionaries to watch the body of the girl during the night. Hyde recorded,

> November 1st. Labored some after striving awhile in the morning having set up all night with the dead, went up to S. Waymouth 5 miles during the day and tarried all night 2nd went down to W.

Drunnets and preached a funeral sermon at 2 o'clock in the afternoon, had a very solemn time and the Lord was with us in some degree attended the burial with much solemnity had a prayer and conference meeting in the evening two or three seemed to have some life, but rather dull meeting, but I think it was productive of some good. I ... returned back to William Drunnets and labored with them and brought them a little nearer the kingdom.[13]

In November, the missionaries again talked with William Drunnets, after which he "concluded to be baptized." They traveled three miles to South Waymouth and baptized him. In the evening, they "had prayers and very good time, and the Lord was with us and Satan also came in a crazy sort of a female, we cried against her and after a short time got her still, tarried at the same place."[14]

Though the missionaries never reached Portland, their original destination, the work began to take root in York County with the establishment of a branch on 9 November 1832 at Lyman. A small branch of the Church was organized in Saco, near Lyman, during the same time. Although the first missionary labors did not expand beyond York County, other missionaries spread the message farther north and ultimately reached the islands off the coast of Maine.

Fox Islands, Maine

The Fox Islands, now known as North Haven (North Fox Island) and Vinalhaven (South Fox Island), are located approximately seventy-five miles north of Portland, Maine. The islands are approximately thirteen miles off the coast of Maine opposite the coastal town of Rockland.

Approximately sixty islands are in the North and South Fox Islands archipelago. The islands received their name from the so-called silver foxes that roamed the islands. Apparently, the islands were permanently settled in 1629; but three countries claimed them—the British, French, and Dutch. The British finally won control.

The Fox Islands were the site of Mormon missionary activities in 1837 by Wilford Woodruff and Jonathan H. Hale and during the winter of 1837–38 by Wilford and Phoebe Woodruff.[15] The missionaries took passage on a steamboat from Bangor, Maine, which carried them to Owl's Head. At Owl's Head, they boarded a sloop that carried them to North Fox Island (North Haven). They arrived at 2:00 a.m. in the morning on 20 August. Surprisingly, they found lodging for the night and in the morning were fed breakfast by a kindly islander. They were not charged for their accommodations. Woodruff wrote, "I then asked her if there was any minister or church on the island. She informed us that there was a Baptist minister, named Newton, who had a congregation and a meeting house about five miles from here."[16]

The two missionaries traveled to the church just before a meeting was about to begin. They were invited to come in and to sit beside the minister. After his sermon, Newton asked them what they wanted. They responded that they wanted him to announce a preaching meeting. The Baptist minister told his congregation that the two strangers would be present at the building at 5:00 p.m. in the evening to deliver their message. He then invited them to return home with him before the meeting. Woodruff wrote,

> Elder Hale and I went to the stand, and I arose with peculiar feelings and addressed the congregation for one hour, taking for my text Galatians 1:8-9. This was the first time that I, or any other elder of the Church of Jesus Christ of Latter Day Saints, had (to my knowledge) attempted to preach the fulness of the gospel and the Book of

North Haven, Fox Islands, Maine
(Wilford Woodruff visited here in 1837–38)
Photograph courtesy of North Haven Historical Society — Unknown, ca. 1890

Mormon to the inhabitants of any island of the sea. I had much liberty in speaking, and informed the people that the Lord had raised up a prophet and organized His Church as in the days of Christ and the ancient apostles, with prophets, apostles, and the gifts as anciently, and that he had brought forth the Book of Mormon. At the close of my remarks Elder Hale bore testimony.[17]

During the next thirteen days, Woodruff and Hale delivered seventeen discourses. On 21 August, Woodruff recorded,

Visited the sea shore, We saw twenty gallant ships under sail. It was a fine day. We went to the North District and preached in the school house. Elder Hale spake upon the authenticity of the Book of Mormon. I followed him. The Spirit of GOD rested upon us. We spent the night with Mr. Stephen Luce.[18]

The work continued successfully as the missionaries spread the message of the restoration across the islands. On 22 August, Woodruff recorded their activities by saying, "walked to the South School and I preached to a large Congregation. Priest Newton was among the number. I was clothed with much of the Spirit of God. We spent the night at Mr. Benjamin Kents. Distance 8 Miles." Eventually, Woodruff and

District Northeast School, Fox Islands, Maine
(Wilford Woodruff preached here in 1837–38)
Photograph courtesy of North Haven Historical Society — Unknown, unknown

Hale divided their work; and on some occasions, one would preach at one school and the other at another school on the same night. On 27 August, Woodruff recorded,

> I walked to the East Parish and found Elder Hale. I preached at 10 a.m. on Faith. I also preached in the Baptist meeting house to a large congregation at 5 p.m. on the coming of Christ, and gave out five appointments for the week. While I had a congregation during the day, I was credibly informed, that Mr. Newton had not one soul besides himself to attend his meeting.

Baptist Church, Fox Islands, Maine
(Wilford Woodruff preached here in 1837–38)
Photograph courtesy of North Haven Historical Society — Unknown, ca. 1868

Though Newton rejected the message, Woodruff noted,

We commenced baptizing his flock . . . We continued to baptize the people on north Island until we baptized every person who owned an interest in the Baptist meeting-house. I then followed Mr. Douglas [Methodist minister who came to put down "Mormonism" at the invitation of Newton] home to South Island, and preached the gospel to the members of his church, and baptized nearly all of them.[19]

The Mormon mission to the islands certainly had an effect. A Baptist Church record dated 19 January 1838 states, "At Church meeting excluded Nathaniel Thomas and his wife and Ruth Luce from the Church having joined the Mormons." The *North Island* states that for "the years 1835 to 1837 total church membership shrank from 134 to 54 members."[20]

Eventually, Woodruff and Hale organized branches of the Church on both islands and departed on 2 October 1837, having baptized almost 100 individuals. Elder Hale proceeded home to Kirtland, Ohio, while Woodruff remained for a short time at Scarborough, Maine, visiting family and friends. During the winter months of 1837–38, Wilford and his wife Phoebe returned to the islands several times to continue their missionary labors. While on the mainland, Woodruff preached in the communities of Scarborough, Bangor, Searsmont, Camden, and Belfast, Maine. The Saints on the Fox Islands and on the mainland followed Woodruff toward the Mormon Zion soon thereafter.

RHODE ISLAND

Rhode Island was founded in the 1630s by William Coddington, Anne Hutchinson, and Roger Williams. They were religious dissenters from the Massachusetts Colony. From the beginning of its existence, Rhode Island spawned religious liberty and a division between church and state.

By the 1650s, Rhode Island was an important part of New England's maritime economy. Because it was so dependent upon this aspect of commerce, Rhode Island was highly sensitive to the economic policies of the English crown. In 1765, a mob in Newport destroyed a boat from a British warship to protest the impressment of Rhode Island seamen. At least two British revenue ships were destroyed in 1769 and 1777 as yet another protest against British policies.

During the Revolutionary War, the British army occupied Newport. The only significant battle in Rhode Island during the war was the failed attempt to dislodge the occupying troops from Newport. Other towns, including Providence, escaped the ravages of war and as a result were able to sustain their growth, both economically and numerically.

Following the war, Rhode Island established the first water-powered textile mill in America. Throughout the nineteenth century, Rhode Island was among the largest textile producers in the country.

On 13 July 1832, Orson Hyde and Samuel H. Smith arrived in Rhode Island during their missionary tour through New England. They contacted some friends and baptized their first convert on 18 July 1832. Their missionary efforts in Rhode Island did not meet with total success; they barely escaped falling into the hands of a mob on several occasions.

Balloon View, Providence, Rhode Island
(Site of early missionary activity—looking south)
Photo courtesy of the Museum of Modern Art—James E. Black, 1860

They continued on the trip, visiting other New England states after they left Rhode Island on 25 July 1832. During the next few years, a branch was organized at Newport and Providence. In 1835,

Church members in Rhode Island wrote Church leaders in Ohio requesting a visit by missionaries to their area. As a result, an announcement was printed in the Church newspaper, *Messenger and Advocate*:

> Our brethren residing in R. I. besides business of a temporal nature request some of the elders to call on them if passing. Brother M. Wilber writes as follows: "April 5th, I baptized 2 persons, and there are more who expect to go forward soon: things appear more encouraging then heretofore—will you invite some of the first elders this way, to see us this season? as we understand they are coming to the east. Direct them to *Providence* R. I. No. 286 North Main St. We will try to have a place for them, where they may instruct the people, if possible—We want to be instructed more perfectly in the things of God."[1]

Oliver Cowdery, a Church leader from Kirtland, Ohio, visited Providence in the late summer of 1836. He wrote,

> At about 7, A.M. we entered the mouth of Providence River, on the east bank of which our Government is erecting or preparing a large

Providence, Rhode Island
(Oliver Cowdery and Brigham Young visited here in 1837)
Photograph courtesy of the Rhode Island Historical Society —James E. Black, 1860

fortification . . . Near to, and on the same side of the river with Fort Adams, stands the *old* town of New Port . . . Thirty miles from this stands the city of Providence . . . Providence, this day, was literally *alive*: it was the anniversary of their town and State—two hundred years had elapsed since its settlement. [2]

While his stay was short, other missionaries during the same time arrived in Rhode Island to conduct Church business and continue the work of spreading the cause of the Church. Brigham Young and his brother, Joseph Young, arrived in Rhode Island from Boston in August 1836. Brigham recorded,

We started [from Boston] for Kirtland, stopped at Providence, R. I. tarried a short time and preached to the Saints and others who came to hear us, then proceeded on our journey through Rhode Island.[3]

Other missionaries arrived in Rhode Island during the 1830s, including Truman Angell, who was born at North Providence in 1810. Both Nathan and Rhoda Lapham Harris, Martin Harris' parents, were born in Rhode Island as was also John Tanner.

EPILOGUE

Shortly after the Church was organized in New York on 6 April 1830, a quarterly Church conference was held at the Whitmer farm in January 1831. Joseph Smith's history reports,

> The year 1831 opened with a prospect great and glorious for the welfare of the Kingdom; for on 2nd of January, 1831 a conference was held in the town of Fayette, New York, at which the ordinary business of the Church was transacted.[1]

A revelation about the move to Ohio became the focus of the Saints' attention during the next weeks and months.[2] The revelation promised the new converts "greater riches, even a land of promise, a land flowing with milk and honey, upon which there shall be no curse when the Lord cometh; And I will give it unto you for the land of your inheritance, if you seek with all your heart."[3]

The precise location of this promised land was not identified in the revelation. For the moment, though, the Saints were to gather in Ohio where the Law of the Lord was to be revealed and where an endowment of power was to be received.

The move to the Western Reserve had several other immediate benefits to the New York Saints. First, the members hoped that the severe persecution, particularly in the Colesville area, would be left behind in New York. In addition, the greatest number of Saints were now in Ohio after a very successful missionary effort earlier in the fall. Nevertheless, the most important reason for such a move was the belief that Kirtland, Ohio, was a step closer to the land of Missouri, where the Saints were promised Zion would be revealed.

194

Through the winter and early spring of 1831, several members, including Joseph and Emma Smith, made their way to Kirtland, Ohio, in the Western Reserve. By the end of June 1831, the majority of New York Saints had left their homes and migrated to the new Church headquarters in Ohio.

As the Church gathering place moved from New York to Ohio to Missouri and to Illinois, leaders and missionaries continued to crisscross back through the Northeastern States in subsequent years, contacting friends and family members and preaching the restored gospel publicly in courthouses, churches, school houses, barns, or wherever they could obtain a hearing. But New York and New England would never play the same role in the Church that they had once played during the birth of Mormonism.

The Mack farm in Vermont, the Smith home in New Hampshire, the Sacred Grove in New York, and the Susquehanna River in Pennsylvania were all left behind. Their importance for the beginnings of the Church remained, but they were abandoned so the Saints could gather and build their Zion in the West.

Eventually, decades later, many Saints returned to the Northeastern States on pilgrimages to the area where Mormonism was born. Among those who came to the Church historical sites located in the Northeastern United States were photographers. The most celebrated was George Edward Anderson of Springville, Utah. A few of his photographic images were published in a Boston newspaper, and a larger collection was published by the LDS Church's Sunday School organization in a book entitled *The Birth of Mormonism in Picture, Scenes and Incidents, in Early Church History*. The editors added these words of explanation to their publication:

> The Birth of Mormonism in Pictures *was* undertaken from two motives: first, a desire to preserve in attractive form photographs of places that will always be revered by Latter-day Saints; and second, a wish to tell in a new way the wonderful story of that birth.[4]

Appendix One

SITE INFORMATION

The political subdivisions in the Northeastern United States can be confusing for those who are not familiar with the use of the term *"town."* The term does not mean city, hamlet, or village. *Town* is the shortened form of *township*. A township is the subsection of a county and usually contains several villages or communities, one of which frequently bears the name of the township. For example, Windsor County, Vermont, is composed of twenty-four townships (towns). One of the towns in Windsor County is Sharon. To say Joseph Smith, Jr. was born in Sharon does not mean that he was born in the village of Sharon but rather the township of Sharon. Most of the sites discussed in this book are located in townships, not villages.

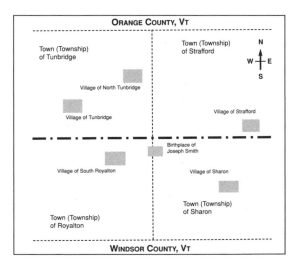

The following list identifies some of the sites discussed in this book that still have the original (reconstructed or restored) structure or marker at the site.

Topsfield, Massachusetts — Smith Family Marker (Pine Grove Cemetery)

Salem, Massachusetts — Peabody Museum; Lyceum Hall

Boston, Massachusetts — Commercial Street Meeting House

Tunbridge, Vermont — Village Store; North Tunbridge; Universalist Meeting House

Sharon, Vermont — Joseph Smith, Sr. Home Site (marker); Joseph Smith, Jr. Monument; LDS Church Visitors Center; Solomon Mack Home Site (marker and foundation); Daniel Mack Home Site (marker and foundation); Old Stone Bridge (marker)

Norwich, Vermont — Joseph Smith Farm (Squire Murdock Farm)

Whitingham, Vermont — Brigham Young Marker (Town Hill Park); Brigham Young Marker (Brigham Young/Stimpson Hill)

Wells, Vermont — William Cowdery Home Site (marker and foundation)

Sheldon, Vermont — Heber C. Kimball Marker (Sheldon Creek Cemetery)

Hanover, New Hampshire — Dartmouth College

Manchester, New York — Joseph Smith, Sr. Home; Sacred Grove; District School Site (Cobble Stone building and marker); District School (Original Frame); Hill Cumorah; Angel Moroni Monument; LDS Church Visitors Center

Palmyra, New York — E. B. Grandin Book Store; John Swift Memorial Cemetery (Alvin Smith tombstone); Palmyra Cemetery (various tombstones); Martin Harris Farm (marker); Erie Canal (Canal Park)

Fishers, New York — Phineas Howe Young Home

Mendon, New York — John Young Home; Tomlinson Inn; Tomlinson Corner Cemetery; Solomon Kimball Home

Fayette, New York — Peter Whitmer, Sr. Home; LDS Church Visitors Center

South Bainbridge (Afton), New York — Squire Tarbell Home Site (marker)

Harmony, Pennsylvania — Joseph Smith, Jr. Home Site (marker); Priesthood Restoration Monument; McKune Cemetery (various tombstones)

Avon, Connecticut — Avon West Cemetery (various tombstones); Lot Thompson Home; Lovely Street School

Appendix Two

PHOTOGRAPHIC SOURCES

The following list identifies information regarding the photographs used in this book.

Avon Historical Society. Avon, Connecticut. Local history and photograph collection of Avon, Connecticut. Contact person: Gladys August.

Barry, Charlotte. Tunbridge, Vermont. She is the current owner of the Tunbridge Village Store and has a private collection of a few old photographs of the store.

Black, Susan Easton. Provo, Utah. Collection contains numerous photographs of cemetery gravestones from her biographical research.

Boston Public Library. Boston, Massachusetts. Collection includes photographs and illustrations of Boston, Massachusetts.

Bostonian Society (The Boston Historical Society and Museum). Boston, Massachusetts. Collection includes photographs and illustrations of Boston.

Brigham Young University, Harold B. Lee Library Archives. Provo, Utah. Collection includes material and photographs of LDS Church history.

Buffalo and Erie County Historical Society. Buffalo, New York. Collection includes local history, photographs, and illustrations of Buffalo and Erie Counties, including Niagara Falls.

California Museum of Photography. Riverside, California. Collection includes the Keystone Stereo-view material (James Ricalton photographs).

The Church of Jesus Christ of Latter-day Saints, Church Education System College Curriculum Department. Salt Lake City, Utah. Collection includes a wide range of photographs relating to LDS Church history.

The Church of Jesus Christ of Latter-day Saints, Historical Department. Salt Lake City, Utah. Large holdings include George Edward Anderson Collection, photo album presented to Joseph F. Smith by George E. Anderson, Brigham Young Slide Collection, Junius F. Wells Collection, Daniel Shupe Collection, Robert Spence Collection, Harry Allsworth Collection, and Joseph F. Smith Memorial Dedication Trip Collection.

The Church of Jesus Christ of Latter-day Saints, Visual Resources Library. Salt Lake City, Utah. Collection includes recent color photographs and slides of LDS Church history sites.

Columbia University. New York City, New York. Collection includes photographs and illustrations of Columbia College and University.

Dartmouth College. Hanover, New Hampshire. Collection includes photographs and illustrations of Dartmouth College and Hanover, New Hampshire.

Essex Institute. Salem, Massachusetts. Collection includes local history, photographs, and illustrations of Salem, Massachusetts.

Fisher, Sheldon. Rochester, New York. Collection contains several photographs of Mormon sites in and around Fishers and Mendon, New York.

The Historical Society of Pennsylvania. Philadelphia, Pennsylvania. Collection includes local history, photographs, and illustrations of Pennsylvania.

The Museum of Modern Art. New York City, New York. Collection includes modern art and several early photographs of sites on the East Coast.

New York Historical Society. New York City, New York. Collection includes local history, photographs, and illustrations of New York City.

Nintzel, Jeffery. Plainfield, New Hampshire. He is a professional photographer and has a private collection of local historic sites in New Hampshire.

North Haven Historical Society. North Haven, Maine. Collection includes local history and photographs of the islands.

Old York Historical and Improvement Society. York, Maine. Collection includes local history and a small photographic and sketch collection of York, Maine.

Park, Stewart. Wells, Vermont. He is currently president of the Wells Historical Society. He has a private collection of photographs of Wells, Vermont.

Peabody Museum of Salem. Salem, Massachusetts. Collection includes local history, photographs, and illustrations of Salem, Massachusetts.

Perrysburg Historical Society. Perrysburg, New York. Collection includes local history and photographs of Perrysburg. Contact person: Lorraine Marvin, Gowanda, New York.

Rich, Margaret. Orem, Utah. She has a private collection of of Church historical sites taken by her late husband, Dr. Russell R. Rich.

Rhode Island Historical Society. Providence, Rhode Island. Collection includes photographs and illustrations of Rhode Island.

Rochester Public Library, Local History Division. Rochester, New York. Collection includes local history, photographs, and illustrations of Rochester, New York.

Sheldon Historical Society. Sheldon, Vermont. Collection includes local history and photographs of Sheldon, Vermont. Contact person: Susan Burnor, Town Clerk's Office.

South Royalton Historical Society. South Royalton, Vermont. Collection includes local history and photographs of South Royalton. Contact person: John Dumville.

Topsfield Historical Society. Topsfield, Massachusetts. Collection includes local history and photographs of Topsfield. Contact person: J. Jan Jansen.

Tunbridge Historical Society. Tunbridge, Massachusetts. Collection includes local history and photographs of Tunbridge. Contact person: Euclid Farnham.

United States Department of Agriculture, National Archives and Record Service, Cartographic and Architectural Branch. Washington, D.C. Collection contains aerial photographs of any location in the United States.

Utah State Historical Society. Salt Lake City, Utah. Collection includes Utah State history and photographs of LDS Church historical sites.

Wells Historical Society. Wells, Vermont. Collection includes local history and photographs of Wells, Vermont. Contact person: Stewart Park.

NOTES

Preface

1. William Cupp Darrah, *Stereo Views: A History of Stereographs in America and Their Collection* (Gettysburg: Times and News Publishing Co., 1964), 167.

2. John K. Carmack, "Fayette: The Place the Church Was Organized," *Ensign* 19 (February 1989):17.

Early History of Joseph Smith and the Church

1. Journal of George Edward Anderson, 20 April 1907, Archives, Historical Department, The Church of Jesus Christ of Latter-day Saints, Salt Lake City, Utah, [hereafter cited as LDSCA].

2. Ibid., 29 June 1907.

3. Ibid., 13 and 17 August 1907.

4. John Henry Evans, *The Birth of Mormonism in Picture: Scenes and Incidents in Early Church History* (Salt Lake City: Deseret Sunday School Union, 1909).

5. Journal of George Edward Anderson, 25 April 1907.

6. Ibid., 20 August 1907.

7. See Whitney R. Cross, *The Burned-over District* (Ithaca: Cornell University Press, 1982).

8. Quoted in Nelson Wadsworth, "A Village Photographer's Dream," *Ensign* 3 (September 1973):55.

9. Journal of George Edward Anderson, 18 August 1907.

10. Ibid., 23 April 1907.

11. Ibid., 24 April 1907.

12. Ibid., 25–26 April 1907.

13. Ibid., 27 April 1907.

14. Ibid., 7 August 1907.

15. *Journal of Discourses*, 26 vols. (London: Latter-day Saints' Book Depot, 1854–86; reprinted 1967) 18:132.

16. Journal of George Edward Anderson, 16 May 1907.

17. Ibid.

18. Ibid., 22 May 1907.

19. Ibid., 1 May 1907.

20. Ibid., 3 May 1907.

21. Ibid.

22. Quoted in Fawn M. Brodie, *No Man Knows My History: The Life of Joseph Smith*, 2nd ed. (New York: Alfred A. Knopf, Inc. 1971), 397.

23. Journal of George Edward Anderson, 4 May 1907.

24. See Steven L. Shields, *The Latter Day Saint Churches: An Annotated Bibliography* (New York: Garland Publishing, Inc., 1987).

Massachusetts

1. Quoted in Elizabeth K. Ritchie, "Aurelia S. Rogers," *Sister Saints*, Vicky Burgess-Olson, ed. (Provo: Brigham Young University Press, 1978), 225.

2. Ibid., 226.

3. See Donald Q. Cannon, "Topsfield, Massachusetts: Ancestral Home of the Prophet Joseph Smith," *BYU Studies* 13 (Autumn 1973):56–76.

4. Quoted in Richard L. Anderson, *Joseph Smith's New England Heritage* (Salt Lake City: Deseret Book Company, 1971), 89–91.

5. Ibid., 98–99.

6. Ibid., 91.

7. "George A. Smith," *Contributor* 4 (October 1882):3.

8. Quoted in Donald Q. Cannon, "Joseph Smith in Salem," *Studies in Scripture: The Doctrine and Covenants*, Robert L. Millet and Kent P. Jackson, eds. (Salt Lake City: Randall Book, 1984), 432.

9. Ibid., 434.

10. Album for the Use of Visitors, 9 August 1836, Peabody Museum Library, Salem, Massachusetts.

11. Quoted in Donald Q. Cannon, "Joseph Smith in Salem," 436.

12. This tract is reprinted in *The Essential Parley P. Pratt*, Introduction by Peter L. Crawley (Midvale: Signature Books, Inc., 1990), 131–40.

13. Parley P. Pratt, *Autobiography of Parley P. Pratt* (Salt Lake City: Deseret Book Company, 1973), 290.

14. *Times and Seasons*, 16 May 1842.

15. See Dean May, "Boston's Mormon Landmark: Abijah Tewkesbury's Office," *Ensign* 3 (November 1973):17–19.

16. Elden Jay Watson, ed., *Manuscript History of Brigham Young, 1801–1844* (Salt Lake City: Smith Secretarial Services, 1968), 149.

17. Ibid., 150.

18. Journal of H. Larkin Southworth, 19 February 1843, LDSCA.

Vermont

1. Quoted in Richard L. Anderson, *New England Heritage*, 112.

2. Quoted in Andrew Karl Larson, *Erastus Snow: The Life of a Missionary and Pioneer for the Early Mormon Church* (Salt Lake City: University of Utah Press, 1971), 2.

3. *The Doctrine and Covenants of The Church of Jesus Christ of Latter-day Saints* (Salt Lake City: The Church of Jesus Christ of Latter-day Saints, 1985): 75 [hereafter cited as LDS D&C]; *Book of Doctrine and Covenants* (Independence: Herald Publishing House, 1989):74 [hereafter cited as RLDS D&C].

4. Elden Jay Watson, comp., *The Orson Pratt Journals* (Salt Lake City: Elden Jay Watson, 1975), 12.

5. Ibid., 16.

6. Quoted in Richard L. Anderson, *New England Heritage*, 124–29.

7. See Richard L. Bushman, *Joseph Smith and the Beginnings of Mormonism* (Urbana: University of Illinois Press, 1984).

8. Lucy Mack Smith, *History of Joseph Smith by His Mother, Lucy Mack Smith*, Preston Nibley, ed. (Salt Lake City: Bookcraft, 1954), 43.

9. Lucy Mack Smith, *History of Joseph Smith*, 31.

10. Ibid., 32.

11. Quoted in "The Way It Looks Today: A Camera Tour of Church History Sites in New England, New York, Pennsylvania, and Ohio," *Ensign* 8 (September 1978):39.

12. Quoted in Larry C. Porter, "A Study of the Origins of the Church of Jesus Christ in the States of New York and Pennsylvania, 1816–1831," Ph.D. diss., Brigham Young University, 1971, 19.

13. Lucy Mack Smith, *History of Joseph Smith*, 46.

14. Ibid.

15. *Proceedings at the Dedication of the Joseph Smith Memorial Monument*, (Salt Lake City: Historical Department, The Church of Jesus Christ of Latter-day Saints, n.d.), 26.

16. Lucy Mack Smith, *History of Joseph Smith*, 47.

17. See Henry and Elizabeth Stommel, "The Year Without Summer," *Scientific American* 240 (June 1979):176–86.

18. Lucy Mack Smith, *History of Joseph Smith*, 59.

19. Quoted in Leonard J. Arrington and Joann Jolly, "The Faithful Young Family: The Parents, Brothers and Sisters of Brigham," *Ensign* 10 (August 1980):53.

20. See Larry C. Porter, "Brigham Young's Birthplace in Whitingham, Vermont," *Regional Studies in Latter-day Saint Church History* (Provo: Department of Church History and Doctrine, 1988), 65–84.

21. Quoted in Eugene England, *Brother Brigham* (Salt Lake City: Bookcraft, 1980), 2.

22. Quoted in Eugene England, *Brother Brigham*, 2.

New Hampshire

1. Quoted in Richard L. Anderson, *New England Heritage*, 147–148.
2. Journal of Orson Hyde, 17–18 October 1832, LDSCA.
3. Lucy Mack Smith, *History of Joseph Smith* p.51.
4. Ibid., 56.
5. Quoted in LeRoy S. Wirthlin, "Nathan Smith (1762–1828) Surgical Consultant to Joseph Smith," *BYU Studies* 17 (Spring 1977):320.
6. Quoted in LeRoy S. Wirthlin, "Nathan Smith," *BYU Studies*, 325.
7. Lucy Mack Smith, *History of Joseph Smith*, 51.

New York

1. Quoted in Hyrum L. Andrus and Helen Mae Andrus, *They Knew the Prophet* (Salt Lake City: Bookcraft, 1974), 1.
2. Quoted in *Church History In the Fulness of Times* (Salt Lake City: The Church of Jesus Christ of Latter-day Saints, 1989), 42.
3. Joseph Smith History 1:63, in *The Pearl of Great Price* (Salt Lake City: The Church of Jesus Christ of Latter-day Saints, 1986) [hereafter cited as JS-History].
4. Ibid., 1:64.
5. Quoted in Wilford C. Wood, *Joseph Smith Begins His Work* (Salt Lake City: Wilford C. Wood, 1958), Introduction.
6. Lucy Mack Smith, *History of Joseph Smith*, 166.
7. Journal of William Hyde, LDSCA.
8. Quoted in William Mulder and A. Russel Mortensen, *Among the Mormons* (New York: Alfred A. Knopf, 1969), 28.
9. Dean C. Jessee, "Joseph Knight's Recollection of Early Mormon History," *BYU Studies* 17 (Autumn 1976):37.
10. Quoted in Richard L. Anderson, *Investigating the Book of Mormon Witnesses* (Salt Lake City: Deseret Book, 1981), 11–12.
11. *The Reflector*, 1 June 1830.
12. Lucy Mack Smith, *History of Joseph Smith*, 169–70.
13. LDS D&C 20/RLDS D&C 17.
14. LDS D&C 42/RLDS D&C 42.
15. See Robert J. Matthews, *"A Plainer Translation": Joseph Smith's Translation of the Bible* (Provo: Brigham Young University Press, 1975).
16. LDS D&C 38:28/RLDS D&C 38:6b.
17. LDS D&C 38:31–32/RLDS D&C 38:7a–b.
18. LDS D&C 84:112–114/RLDS D&C 83:23.
19. Quoted in Dean C. Jessee, ed., *The Personal Writings of Joseph Smith* (Salt Lake City: Deseret Book Company, 1983), 252.
20. Ibid., 253–54.
21. Ibid., 18.

22. Quoted in Lyndon W. Cook, *The Revelations of the Prophet Joseph Smith* (Provo: Seventy's Mission Bookstore, 1981), 203.

23. LDS D&C 100:1–4/RLDS D&C 97:1a–c.

24. Quoted in Parley P. Pratt, *Autobiography*, 110.

25. Ibid.

26. Ibid., 110–11.

27. Ibid., 111.

28. Quoted in Janet Peterson and La Rene Gaunt, *Elect Ladies* (Salt Lake City: Deseret Book Company, 1990), 43.

29. Ibid., 47.

30. Lucy Mack Smith, *History of Joseph Smith*, 199–205.

31. Quoted in Donald L. Enders, "A Snug Little House," *Ensign* 15 (August 1985):16.

32. Lucy Mack Smith, *History of Joseph Smith*, 85.

33. Ibid., 108–12.

34. Ibid., 189.

35. JS-History 1:4.

36. Quoted in Milton V. Backman, *Joseph Smith's First Vision: The First Vision in Its Historical Context,* 2nd ed. rev. (Salt Lake City: Bookcraft, 1980), 159.

37. Quoted in Milton V. Backman, *First Vision*, 168–69.

38. Lucy Mack Smith, *History of Joseph Smith*, 138–39.

39. Quoted in Dean C. Jessee, *Personal Writings*, 6–7.

40. See Larry C. Porter, "Origins of the Church of Jesus Christ," 68–70.

41. *Messenger and Advocate*, October 1835.

42. Quoted in Larry C. Porter, "Origins of the Church of Jesus Christ," 70.

43. Quoted in Wilford Wood, *Joseph Smith Begins His Work*, Introduction.

44. *The Reflector*, 2 January 1830.

45. Quoted in "The Coming Forth of the Book of Mormon," *Ensign* 13 (December 1983):44.

46. *Wayne Sentinel*, 30 September 1824.

47. "John H. Gilbert Statement," LDSCA.

48. Lucy Mack Smith, *History of Joseph Smith*, 130–31.

49. Quoted in "The Coming Forth of the Book of Mormon," 49.

50. LDS D&C 37:1/RLDS D&C 37:1a.

51. Lucy Mack Smith, *History of Joseph Smith*, 195–99.

52. "History of Brigham Young," *Millennial Star* 25 (1863):327, 360–61.

53. Quoted in Leonard J. Arrington, *Brigham Young: American Moses* (New York City: Alfred Knopf, 1985), 17.

54. *Deseret News*, 7 April 1858.

55. "History of Brigham Young," *Millennial Star* 25 (1863):360–61.

56. *Journal of Discourses* 6:132.

57. Elden Jay Watson, *Manuscript History of Brigham Young 1801–1844*, 3.

58. *The Saints' Herald*, 1 March 1882.

59. *A Book of Commandments* 4:4, reprint ed. (Independence: Herald House, 1972).

60. *The Saints' Herald*, 1 March 1882.

61. LDS D&C 14–18, 20–21, 28–31, 33–36, and 38–40/RLDS D&C 12–16, 17,19, 27–30, 31–34 32–35, and 38–40.

62. *Journal of Discourses* 7:372.

63. Lucy Mack Smith, *History of Joseph Smith*, 93.

64. Quoted in Larry C. Porter, "The Colesville Branch and the Coming Forth of the Book of Mormon," *BYU Studies* 10 (Spring 1970):381.

65. Quoted in Larry C. Porter, "Origins of the Church of Jesus Christ," 183.

66. Quoted in William Hartley, *They Are My Friends: A History of the Joseph Knight Family, 1825–1850* (Provo: Grandin Book Company, 1986), 206.

67. Broome County *Republican*, 5 May 1831.

Pennsylvania

1. Quoted in Michael S. Durham, *The Smithsonian Guide to Historic America (Mid-Atlantic States)* (New York: Stewart, Tabori, and Chang, 1989), 326.

2. Ibid.

3. Joseph Smith, Jr., *History of The Church of Jesus Christ of Latter-day Saints*, B.H. Roberts, ed., 2nd ed. rev. 7 vols. (Salt Lake City: Deseret News, 1932–51) 4:47 [hereafter cited *History of the Church*].

4. Ibid., 4:48.

5. Ibid., 4:49.

6. Ibid., 4:77.

7. Ibid., 4:224.

8. Quoted in Dean C. Jessee, *Personal Writings*, 207.

9. Quoted in Larry C. Porter, "Origins of the Church of Jesus Christ," 115.

10. Ibid., 133.

11. *Messenger and Advocate*, October 1834.

12. Ibid.

13. LDS D&C 13.

14. Quoted in E. D. Howe, *Mormonism Unveiled* (Painesville: for the author, 1834), 234.

15. JS-History 1:18.

16. *Messenger and Advocate*, October 1834.

Connecticut

1. Quoted in "Joseph Smith, The Prophet," *Young Women's Journal* 16 (December 1905):553.

2. Quoted in Matthias F. Cowley, *Wilford Woodruff: History of His Life and Labors* (Salt Lake City: Bookcraft, 1964), 4.

3. Scott G. Kenney, ed., *Wilford Woodruff's Journal: 1833–1898, Typescript*, 9 vols. (Midvale: Signature Books, 1983) 1:159–60.

4. Ibid., 1:161.

5. Ibid., 1:162.

6. Ibid., 1:160.

7. Matthias F. Cowley, *Wilford Woodruff*, 9.

8. Scott G. Kenney, *Wilford Woodruff's Journals*, 1:162.

9. Ibid., 1:163.

10. Ibid., 1:262.

11. Matthias F. Cowley, *Wilford Woodruff*, 7.

12. Scott G. Kenney, *Wilford Woodruff's Journals*, 1:162.

13. Ibid., 1:163.

14. Ibid., 1:161.

Maine

1. Quoted in Susan Sessions Rugh, "Patty B. Sessions," in *Sister Saints*, 306.

2. *Messenger and Advocate*, October 1834.

3. LDS D&C 75/RLDS D&C 74.

4. Journal of Orson Hyde, 19 October 1832, LDSCA.

5. Ibid.

6. Ibid., 21–22 October 1832.

7. Ibid., 23 October 1832.

8. Ibid., 24 October 1832.

9. Ibid., 25 October 1832.

10. Ibid.

11. Journal of Samuel Smith, 25 October 1832, LDSCA.

12. Ibid., 27 October 1832.

13. Journal of Orson Hyde, 1 November 1832.

14. Ibid.

15. See Donald Q.Cannon, "Wilford Woodruff's Mission to the Fox Islands." In *Regional Studies in Latter-day Saints Church History: New England*, Donald Q. Cannon ed. (Provo: Department of Church History and Doctrine, Brigham Young University, 1988), pp. 85–100.

16. Quoted in Matthias F. Cowley, *Wilford Woodruff*, 76.

17. Ibid., 77.

18. Scott G. Kenney, *Wilford Woodruff's Journals*, 1:171.

19. Quoted in Matthias F. Cowley, *Wilford Woodruff*, 78–79.

20. Quoted in Seward E. Beacom, *Silent Fingers of Faith: A History of the Churches of North Haven, Maine* (Rockport: North Haven Historical Society, 1981), 67.

Rhode Island

1. *Messenger and Advocate*, April 1835.

2. Ibid., October 1836.

3. Elden Jay Watson, ed. *Manuscript History of Brigham Young 1801–1844*, 15.

Epilogue

1. *History of the Church*, 1:140.

2. LDS D&C 38/RLDS D&C 38.

3. LDS D&C 38:18–19/RLDS D&C 38.

4. Quoted in Nelson Wadsworth, *Through Camera Eyes* (Provo: Brigham Young University Press, 1975), 167.

SELECTED BIBLIOGRAPHY
OF PUBLISHED MATERIALS

GENERAL AMERICAN HISTORY

Billington, Ray Allen. *Westward Expansion: A History of the American Frontier*. Holt, Rinehart and Winston, 1966.

Bushman, Richard L. "Family Security in the Transition from Farm to City, 1750–1850." In *The Underside of American History*, vol. 1, 315–32. Edited by Thomas R. Frazier. New York: Harcourt Brace Jovanovich, Publishers, 1987.

Pessen, Edward. *Jacksonian America: Society, Personality, and Politics*. Rev. ed. Homewood: The Dorsey Press, 1978.

Riegel, Robert E. *Young America 1830–1840*. Norman: University of Oklahoma Press, 1949.

Russo, David J. *Families and Communities: A New View of American History*. Nashville: The American Association for State and Local History, 1974.

New England/New York/Pennsylvania

Ashton, Dorothy Hemenway. *Sheldon, Vermont: The People Who Lived and Worked There*. St. Albans: Regal Arts Press, 1979.

Blackman, Emily E. *History of Susquehanna County, Pennsylvania*. Philadelphia: Claxton, Remsen and Haffelfinger, 1873.

Chase, Fredrick. *A History of Dartmouth College and the Town of Hanover, New Hampshire to 1815*. Brattleboro: Vermont Printing Company, 1928.

Cook, Edward M. Jr. *The Fathers of the Towns: Leadership and Community Structures in Eighteenth Century New England*. Baltimore: John Hopkins University Press, 1976.

Cross, Whitney R. *The Burned-Over District*. Ithaca: Cornell University Press, 1982.

Dow, George Francis. *History of Topsfield Massachusetts*. Topsfield: The Topsfield Historical Society, 1940. reprint 1982.

Dubler, Alice M. *Manchester Through the Years*. Houghton: Houghton College Press, 1954.

Durham, Michael S. *Smithsonian Guide to Historic America (The Mid-Atlantic States)*. New York: Stewart, Tabori and Chang, 1989.

Ellis, David E., and others. *A Short History of New York State*. New York City: Columbia University Press, 1967.

Hemenway, Abby Maria. *The Vermont Historical Gazetteer*. 4 vols. Burlington: By the Author, 1877–82.

History of Wayne County New York. Philadelphia: Everts, Ensign and Everts, 1877.

Jillson, Clark. *Green Leaves From Whitingham Vermont: A History of the Town*. Worcester: By the Author, 1894.

Ludlum, David M. *Social Ferment in Vermont, 1791–1850*. New York: Columbia University Press, 1939.

MacKie, Mary-Frances L. *Avon, Connecticut: An Historical Story*. Canaan: Phoenix Publishing, 1988.

Muse, Vance. *Smithsonian Guide to Historic America (Northern New England)*. New York: Stewart, Tabori and Chang, 1989.

Palmyra, Wayne County, New York. Rochester: Women's Society of the Western Presbyterian Church, 1907.

Nash, Hope. *Royalton Vermont*. n.p., 1975.

Turner, O. *History of the Pioneer Settlement of Phelps and Gorham's Purchase*. Rochester: William Alling, 1852.

Wells Bi-Centennial Committee. *A Historical Scrapbook: Wells, Vermont, Chartered 1761*. n.p., 1976.

Wienck, Henry. *Smithsonian Guide to Historic America (Southern New England)*. New York: Stewart, Tabori and Chang, 1989.

RELIGION IN AMERICA

Ahlstrom, Sidney, E. *A Religious History of the American People*. New Haven: Yale University Press, 1972.

Allen, James B. "Why Did People Act that Way? Some Observations on Religious Intolerance and Persecution in the American Past." *Ensign* 8 (December 1978):21–24.

Allen, Joseph Henry and Richard Eddy. *A History of Unitarians and Universalists in the United States*. New York: Scribner, 1903.

Backman, Milton V. Jr. *Christian Churches of America: Origins and Beliefs*, Rev. ed. New York: Charles Scribner's Sons, 1983.

_____ . "Preparing the Way: The Rise of Religious Freedom in New England." *Ensign* 19 (January 1989):16–19.

Foster, Lawrence. *Religion and Sexuality: Three American Communal Experiments of the Nineteenth Century*. New York: Oxford University Press, 1981.

Gaustad, Edwing. *A Documentary History of Religion in America to the Civil War*. Grand Rapids: Eerdmans Publishing Company, 1982.

Griffin, C. S. *The Ferment of Reform, 1830–1860*. New York: Thomas Y. Crowell Company, 1967.

Johnson, Charles A. *The Frontier Camp Meeting, Religion's Harvest Time*. Dallas: Southern Methodist University Press, 1955.

McLoughlin, William G. *Revivals, Awakenings, and Reform: An Essay on Religion and Social Change in America, 1607–1977*. Chicago: The University of Chicago Press, 1978.

Mead, Sidney E. "The Fact of Pluralism and the Persistence of Sectarianism." In *The Religion of the Republic*. Edited by Elwyn A. Smith. Philadelphia: Fortress Press, 1974.

Moore, R. Laurence. *Religious Outsiders and the Making of Americans*. New York: Oxford University Press. 1986.

Sweet, William Warren. *Religion in the Development of the American Culture*. New York: Charles Scribner's Sons, 1952.

Weigel, Gustave, S. J. *Churches in North America: An Introduction*. Baltimore: Helicon Press, 1961.

LDS/RLDS CHURCH

General History

Allen, James B., and Glen M. Leonard. *The Story of the Latter-day Saints*. Salt Lake City: Deseret Book, 1976.

Arrington, Leonard J., Davis Bitton. *The Mormon Experience: A History of the Latter-day Saints*. New York: Alfred A. Knopf, 1979.

Backman, Milton V. Jr. *American Religions and the Rise of Mormonism*. Salt Lake City: Deseret Book Company, 1970.

Barrett, Ivan J. *Joseph Smith and the Restoration: A History of the LDS Church to 1846*. Provo: Brigham Young University Press, 1972.

Blair, Alma R. "Reorganized Church of Jesus Christ of Latter Day Saints: Moderate Mormonism." In *The Restoration Movement: Essays in Mormon History*, 207–30. Edited by F. Mark McKiernan, Alma R. Blair and Paul Edwards. Lawrence: Coronado Press, 1973.

Church History in the Fullness of Times: The History of The Church of Jesus Christ of Latter-day Saints. Salt Lake City: The Church of Jesus Christ of Latter-day Saints, 1989.

Howard, Richard P. "Joseph Smith's First Vision: The RLDS Tradition." *Journal of Mormon History* 7 (1980): 23–30.

Launis, Rodger D. "Whither Reorganization Historiography?" *John Whitmer Historical Association Journal* 10 (1990):24–38.

Roberts, B. H. *A Comprehensive History of The Church of Jesus Christ of Latter-day Saints, Century 1*. 6 vols. Salt Lake City: The Church of Jesus Christ of Latter-day Saints, 1930.

Shields, Steven L. *The Latter Day Saint Churches: An Annotated Bibliography*. New York: Garland Publishing, 1986.

Smith, Joseph. *History of The Church of Jesus Christ of Latter-day Saints*. 7 vols. Edited by B. H. Roberts. Salt Lake City: The Church of Jesus Christ of Latter-day Saints, 1932–51.

Smith, Joseph III and Heman C. Smith, eds. *History of the Reorganized Church of Jesus Christ of Latter Day Saints*. 6 vols. Independence: Herald Publishing House, 1973.

Wood, Gordon S. "Evangelical America and Early Mormonism." *New York History* 61 (October 1980):359–86.

LDS in New England/New York/Pennsylvania

Allen, James B. and Leonard Arrington. "Mormon Origins in New York: An Introductory Analysis. *BYU Studies* 9 (Spring 1969):241–274.

Anderson, Lavina Fielding. "Challenge to Greatness: The Nineteenth-Century Saints in New York." *Ensign* 8 (September 1978):25–32.

Arrington, Leonard J. "Mormonism: From Its New York Beginnings." *New York History* 61 (October 1980):387–410.

Backman, Milton V. *Joseph Smith's First Vision*. 2d rev. ed. Salt Lake City: Bookcraft, 1980.

_____ . " The New England Background to the Restoration" In *Regional Studies in Latter-day Saint Church History (New England)*, 33–42. Edited by Donald Q. Cannon. Provo: Department of Church History and Doctrine, Brigham Young University, 1988.

Cannon, Donald Q., ed. *Regional Studies in Latter-day Saint Church History (New England)*. Provo: Department of Church History and Doctrine, Brigham Young University, 1988.

Crawley, Peter. "A Bibliography of The Church of Jesus Christ of Latter-day Saints in New York, Ohio, and Missouri." *BYU Studies* 12 (Summer 1972):465–537.

Davis, David Brion. "The New England Origins of Mormonism." *New England Quarterly* 27 (June 1953):148–53.

Hill, Marvin S. "The Shaping of the Mormon Mind in New England and New York." *BYU Studies* 9 (Spring 1969):351–72.

Porter, Larry C. "The Church in New York and Pennsylvania, 1816–1831." In *The Restoration Movement: Essays in Mormon History*, 27–61 Edited by F. Mark McKiernan, Alma R. Blair, and Paul M. Edwards. Lawrence: Coronado Press, 1973.

BIOGRAPHICAL STUDIES

Anderson, Mary Audentia Smith. *Ancestry and Posterity of Joseph Smith and Emma Hale*. Independence: Herald Publishing House, 1929.

Anderson, Richard L. "The Alvin Smith Story." *Ensign* 17 (August 1987):58–72.

_____ . *Investigating the Book of Mormon Witnesses*. Salt Lake City: Deseret Book, 1981.

_____ . *Joseph Smith's New England Heritage*. Salt Lake City: Deseret Book Company, 1971.

_____ . "Joseph Smith's New York Reputation Reappraised." *BYU Studies* 10 (Spring 1970):283–314.

_____ . "The Mature Joseph Smith and Treasure Searching." *BYU Studies* 24 (Fall 1984):489–560.

_____ . "The Reliability of the Early History of Lucy and Joseph Smith." *Dialogue* 4 (Summer 1969):13–28.

_____ . "What Were Joseph Smith's Sisters Like?" *Ensign* 9 (March 1979): 42–45.

_____ . "The Whitmers." *Ensign* 9 (August 1979):35–40.

Arrington, Leonard J. *Brigham Young: American Moses*. New York: Alfred A. Knopf, 1985.

Arrington, Leonard J. "James Gordon Bennetts: 1831 Report on 'the Mormonites.'" *BYU Studies* 10 (Spring 1970):354–64.

Arrington, Leonard J., and Joann Jolley. "The Faithful Young Family: The Parents, Brothers and Sisters of Brigham." *Ensign* 10 (August 1989):52–57.

Arrington, Leonard J., and Susan Arrington Madsen. "Lucy Mack Smith." In *Mothers of the Prophets*. Salt Lake City: Deseret Book, 1987.

Avery, Valeen T. and Linda K. Newell. *Mormon Enigma: Emma Hale Smith*. Garden City: Doubleday and Company, Inc., 1984.

Barron, Howard H. *Orson Hyde: Missionary, Apostle, Colonizer*. Bountiful: Horizon, 1977.

Black, Susan Easton, comp. *Membership of The Church of Jesus Christ of Latter-day Saints: 1830–48*. Provo: BYU Religious Studies Center, 1989. Fifty volumes.

Brodie, Fawn M. *No Man Knows My History: The Life of Joseph Smith*. New York: Alfred A. Knopf, Inc. 1971.

Bushman, Richard L. *Joseph Smith and the Beginnings of Mormonism*. Urbana: University of Illinois Press, 1984.

Cannon, Donald Q., and David J. Whittaker, eds. *Supporting Saints: Life Stories of Nineteenth-Century Mormons*. Provo: BYU Religious Studies Center, 1985.

Corbett, Pearson H. *Hyrum Smith, Patriarch*. Salt Lake City: Deseret Book, 1963.

Gunn, Stanley R. *Oliver Cowdery, Second Elder and Scribe*. Salt Lake City: Bookcraft, 1962.

Hartley, William G. "The Knight Family: Ever Faithful to the Prophet." *Ensign* 19 (January 1989):43–49.

_____ . *"They Are My Friends," A History of Joseph Knight Family, 1825–1850.* Provo: Grandin Book Company, 1986.

Hayward, Oliver S. "Dr. Nathan Smith (1762–1829) — American Pioneer." *New England Journal of Medicine* 261 (September 1959):489–94.

Hill, Donna. *Joseph Smith: The First Mormon.* Garden City: Doubleday & Company, Inc., 1977.

Jenson, Andrew. *Latter-day Saint Biographical Encyclopedia.* 4 vols. Salt Lake City: Andrew Jenson History Company, 1901.

Jessee, Dean. " 'Steadfastness and Patient Endurance' The Legacy of Edward Partridge." *Ensign* 9 (June 1979):40–47.

Larson, Andrew Karl. *Erastus Snow: The Life of a Missionary and Pioneer for the Early Mormon Church.* Salt Lake City: University of Utah Press, 1971.

Madsen, Truman G. *Joseph Smith the Prophet.* Salt Lake City: Bookcraft, 1989.

Newell, Linda King, and Valeen Tippetts Avery. *Mormon Enigma: Emma Hale Smith.* Garden City: Doubleday & Company, Inc., 1984.

Palmer, Richard F. and Karl D. Butler. *Brigham Young: The New York Years.* Provo: Charles Redd Center for Western Studies, 1982.

Porter, Larry C. "Alvin Smith: Reminder of the Fairness of God." *Ensign* 8 (September 1978):65–67.

_____ . "Reverend George Lane — Good 'Gifts,' Much 'Grace,' and Marked 'Usefulness,' " *BYU Studies* 9 (Spring 1969):321–40.

Pratt, R. Steven. "The 5 Sons of Jared and Charity Pratt." *Ensign* 9 (October 1979):52–57.

Ritchie, Elizabeth Kohler. "Aurelia S. Rogers," In *Sister Saints*, 223–240. Edited by Vicky Burgess-Olson. Provo: Brigham Young University Press, 1978.

Smith, Lucy Mack. *Biographical Sketches of Joseph Smith, the Prophet, and His Progenitors for Many Generations.* Independence: Herald Publishing House, 1969. reprint.

_____ . *History of Joseph Smith.* Edited by Preston Nibley. Salt Lake City: Bookcraft, 1954.

Walker, Ronald W. "Joseph Smith: The Palmyra Seer." *BYU Studies* 24 (Fall 1984):461–72.

_____ . "Martin Harris: Mormonism's Early Convert." *Dialogue* 19 (Winter 1986):29–43.

Wirthlin, LeRoy S. "Nathan Smith (1762–1828): Surgical Consultant to Joseph Smith, *BYU Studies* 17 (Spring 1977):319–38.

CONTEMPORARY ACCOUNTS
AND RECOLLECTIONS

Andrus, Hyrum L., and Helen Mae Andrus, comps. *They Knew the Prophet*. Salt Lake City: Bookcraft, Inc., 1974.

Andrus, Hyrum L., and Richard E. Bennett, eds. *Mormon Manuscripts to 1846: A Guide to the Holdings of the Harold B. Lee Library* Provo: Harold B. Lee Library, Brigham Young University, 1977.

Backman, Milton V. Jr. *Eyewitness Accounts of the Restoration*. Orem: Grandin Book Company, 1983.

Bitton, Davis. *Guide to Mormon Diaries and Autobiographies*. Provo: Brigham Young University Press, 1977.

Clark, James R., ed. *Messages of the First Presidency of The Church of Jesus Christ of Latter-day Saints 1833–1964*. 6 vols. Salt Lake City: Bookcraft, 1964–1965.

Durham, Reed C. "Joseph Smith: Own Story of a Serious Childhood Illness." *BYU Studies* 10 (Summer 1970):480–82.

Faulring, Scott H., ed. *An American Prophet's Record: The Diaries and Journals of Joseph Smith*. Salt Lake City: Signature Books, 1987.

Godfrey, Kenneth W., Audrey M. Godfrey, and Jill Mulvay Derr. *Women's Voices: An Untold History of the Latter-day Saints, 1830–1890*. Salt Lake City: Deseret Book Company, 1982.

Ham, Wayne, ed. *Publish Glad Tidings: Readings in Early Latter-day Saint Sources*. Independence: Herald Publishing House, 1970.

Jessee, Dean C. "Early Accounts of the First Visions" *BYU Studies* 9 (Spring 1969):277–78.

_____. "Joseph Knight's Recollection of Early Mormon History." *BYU Studies* 17 (Autumn, 1976):29–39.

_____. "Joseph Smith, Jr.—In His Own Words, Part 1." *Ensign* 14 (December, 1984):22–31.

_____. "Joseph Smith, Jr.—In His Own Words, Part 2." *Ensign* 15 (January 1985):18–24.

_____. "Joseph Smith, Jr.—In His Own Words, Part 3." *Ensign* 15 (February 1985):6–13.

_____., ed. *The Papers of Joseph Smith: Autobiographical and Historical Writings*. Vol. 1. Salt Lake City: Deseret Book Company 1989.

_____., ed. *The Personal Writings of Joseph Smith*. Salt Lake City: Deseret Book Company, 1983.

Kenney, Scott G., ed. *Wilford Woodruff's Journals: 1833–1898 Typescript*. 9 vols. Midvale: Signature Books, 1983.

Kimball, Stanley B., ed. *On the Potter's Wheel: The Diaries of Heber C. Kimball*. Salt Lake City: Signature Books, 1987.

McKiernan, F. Mark, and Rodger D. Launius. *An Early Latter Day Saint History: The Book of John Whitmer, Kept by Commandment*. Independence: Herald House, 1980.

Mulder, William, and A. Russell Mortensen, eds. *Among the Mormons: Historic Accounts by Contemporary Observers*. New York: Alfred A. Knopf, 1969.

Pratt, Parley P. *Autobiography of Parley P. Pratt*. Salt Lake City; Deseret Book Company, 1973.

Quinn, D. Michael, trans. "The First Months of Mormonism: A Contemporary View by Rev. Diedrich Willers." *New York History* 54 (July 1973):317–33.

"Smith, George A." *Contributor* 4 (October 1882) 1–4.

Watson, Elden Jay, ed. *Manuscript History of Brigham Young, 1801–1844*. Salt Lake City: Smith Secretarial Services, 1968.

Watson, Elden Jay, comp. *The Orson Pratt Journals*. Salt Lake City: Elden Jay Watson, 1975.

DOCTRINAL DEVELOPMENT

Allen, James B. "Emergence of a Fundamental: The Expanding Role of Joseph Smith's First Vision in Mormon Religious Thought." *Journal of Mormon History* 7 (1980):43–61.

_____ . "Line upon Line." *Ensign* 9 (July 1979): 32–39.

Anderson, Richard L. "Joseph Smith and the Millenarian Time Table." *BYU Studies* 3 (Spring-Summer 1961):55–66.

Backman, Milton V. *Joseph Smith's First Vision: The First Vision in Its Historical Context* 2d rev. ed. Salt Lake City: Bookcraft, 1980.

_____ . "Joseph Smith's Recitals of the First Vision." *Ensign* 15 (January 1985):8–17.

Book of Mormon. Joseph Smith, Jr., trans. Palmyra: E. B. Grandin, 1830; Salt Lake City: The Church of Jesus Christ of Latter-day Saints, 1982.

Cannon, Donald Q., Larry E. Dahl, and John W. Welch. "The Restoration of Major Doctrines Through Joseph Smith: Priesthood, The Word of God, and the Temple." *Ensign* 19 (February 1989):7–13.

_____ . "The Restoration of Major Doctrines Through Joseph Smith: The Godhead, Mankind, and The Creation." *Ensign* 19 (January 1989):27–33.

Cook, Lyndon W. *The Revelations of the Prophet Joseph Smith*. Salt Lake City: Deseret Book Company, 1985.

Harrell, Charles R. "The Development of the Doctrine of Preexistence, 1830–1844." *BYU Studies* 28 (Spring 1988):75–96.

Hartley, William G. "Mormon Sundays." *Ensign* 8 (January 1978):19–25.

Howard, Richard P. *Restoration Scriptures: A Study of Their Textual Development*. Independence: Herald Publishing House, 1969.

Irving, Gordon. "The Mormons and the Bible in the 1830s." *BYU Studies* 13 (Summer 1973):473–488.

Journals of Discourses. 26 vols. London: Latter-day Saints' Book Depot, 1854–86; reprinted 1967.

Madsen, Truman G., ed. *Concordance of Doctrinal Statements of Joseph Smith.* Salt Lake City: I.E.F. Publishing, 1985.

Matthews, Robert J. "The 'New Translation' of the Bible, 1830–1833: Doctrinal Development During the Kirtland Era." *BYU Studies* 11 (Summer 1971):400–422.

_____ . *"A Plainer Translation": Joseph Smith's Translation of the Bible; a History and Commentary*. Provo: Brigham Young University Press, 1975.

Smith, Joseph Fielding, comp. *Teachings of the Prophet Joseph Smith.* Salt Lake City: Deseret Book Company, 1961.

Underwood, Grant. "Book of Mormon Usage in Early LDS Theology." *Dialogue* 17 (Autumn 1984):35–74.

_____ . "Millenarianism and the Early Mormon Mind." *Journal of Mormon History*. 9 (1982):41–51.

Woodford, Robert J. "The Doctrine and Covenants: A Historical Overview." In *Studies in Scripture Volume One: Doctrine and Covenants* 3–22. Edited by Robert L. Millet and Kent P. Jackson. Salt Lake City: Randall Book, 1984.

_____ . "How the Revelations in the Doctrine & Covenants were Received and Compiled." *Ensign* 15 (January 1985):26–33.

INDIVIDUAL SITES

Anderson, A. Gary. " The Mack Family and Marlow, New Hampshire". In *Regional Studies in Latter-day Saint Church History (New England)*, 43–52. Edited by Donald Q. Cannon. Provo: Department of Church History and Doctrine, Brigham Young University, 1988.

Anderson, Paul L. "Heroic Nostalgia: Enshrining the Mormon Past. "*Sunstone* 5 (July–August 1980):47–55.

Anderson, Richard L. "The House Where the Church Was Organized." *Improvement Era* 73 (April 1970):16–25.

_____ . "Who were the Six Who Organized the Church on 6 April 1830?" *Ensign* 10 (June 1980):44–95.

Bartschi, Darel P. "The Joseph Smith Memorial: A 1905 Tribute to the Prophet and His Work." *Ensign* 18 (February 1988):7–11.

Berge, Dale L. "Archaeological Work at the Smith Log House." *Ensign* 15 (August 1985):24–26.

_____ . "Archaeology at the Peter Whitmer Farm, Seneca County, New York." *BYU Studies* 13 (Winter 1973):172–201.

Brigham, Janet. "Church History Sites—Separating Fiction and Fact." *Ensign* 9 (March 1979):74–75.

Buchmiller, Golden A. "Grandin Building Opens to Visitors in Palmyra." *Church News* 30 October 1982.

Cannon, Donald Q. "Joseph Smith in Salem," In *Studies in Scripture: The Doctrine and Covenants.* Edited by Robert L. Millet and Kent P. Jacksons. Salt Lake City: Randall Books, 1984.

Cannon, Donald Q. "Topsfield, Massachusetts, Ancestral Home of the Prophet Joseph Smith." *BYU Studies* 13 (Autumn 1973):56–76.

Carmack, John K. "Fayette: The Place the Church Was Organized." *Ensign* 19 (February 1989):14–19.

Enders, Donald L. "The Sacred Grove." *Ensign* 20 (April 1990):14–17.

_____ . "A Snug Log House." *Ensign* 15 (August 1985):14–23.

Fisher, J. Sheldon. "Brigham Young as a Mendon Craftsman: A Study in Historical Archaeology." *New York History* 61 (October 1980):431–47.

Hartley, William G. "Torlief Knaphus, Sculptor Saint." *Ensign* 10 (July 1980):10–15.

"Historic Discoveries at the Grandin Building." *Ensign* 10 (July 1980):48–50.

Kimball, Stanley. "The First Road West From New York to Kirtland, 1831." *Ensign* 9 (January 1979):29–30.

Lyon, T. Edgar. "How Authentic Are Mormon Historic Sites in Vermont and New York," *BYU Studies* 9 (Spring 1969):275–94.

May, Dean. "Boston's Mormon Landmarks: Abijah Tewkesbury's Office" *Ensign* 3 (November 1973):17–19.

"Palmyra: Cradle of the Restoration." *Ensign* 19 (January 1989):38–42.

Rich, Russell. "Where Were the Moroni Visits?" *BYU Studies* 10 (Spring 1970):255–58.

Wells, Junius F. "Potsdam." *The Contributor* 13 (July 1892):377–80.

"Where the Book of Mormon Went to Press." *The Ensign* 19 (February 1989):43–47.

PHOTOGRAPHY

Francis, Rell G. *The Utah Photographs of George Edward Anderson.* Lincoln: University of Nebraska Press, 1979.

Smith, John Henry. *The Birth of Mormonism.* Salt Lake City: Deseret Sunday School Union, 1909.

"The Way it Looks Today: A Camera Tour of Church History Sites in New England, New York, Pennsylvania, and Ohio." *Ensign* 8 (September 1978):33–49.

Tobler, Douglas S., and Nelson B. Wadsworth. *The History of the Mormons in Photographs and Text: 1832 to the Present.* New York: St. Martin Press, 1989.

Wadsworth, Nelson. "A Village Photographer's Dream." *Ensign* 3 (September 1973) 40–55.

SPECIALIZED STUDIES

Allen, James B. "The Significance of Joseph Smith's 'First Vision' in Mormon Thought." *Dialogue* 1 (Autumn 1966):29–45.

Anderson, Richard L. "By the Gift and Power of God." *Ensign* 7 (1977):78–85.

———. "Circumstantial Confirmation of the First Vision Through Reminiscences," *BYU Studies* 9 (Spring 1969):373–404.

———. *Investigating the Book of Mormon Witnesses*. Salt Lake City: Deseret Book Company, 1981.

———. "The Second Witness of Priesthood Restoration." *Improvement Era* 71 (September 1968):15–24.

Bitton, Davis. "Early Mormon Lifestyles: or The Saints as Human Beings." In *The Restoration Movement: Essays in Mormon History,* 273–305. Edited by F. Mack McKiernan, Alma R. Blair, and Paul M. Edwards. Lawrence: Coronado Press, 1973.

Bush, Lester E., Jr. "The Spaulding Theory Then and Now." *Dialogue* 10 (Autumn 1977):40–69.

Bushman, Richard L. "1830: Pivotal Years in the Fullness of Times." *Ensign* 8 (September 1978):9–13.

Bushman, Richard L. "The Book of Mormon in Early Mormon History." In *New Views of Mormon History: Essays in Honor of Leonard J. Arrington,* 3–18. Edited by Davis Bitton and Maureen Ursenbach Beecher. Salt Lake City: University of Utah Press, 1987.

———. "The First Vision Story Revived." *Dialogue* 4 (Spring 1969):82–93.

DePillis, Mario S. "The Quest for Religious Authority and the Rise of Mormonism." *Dialogue* 1 (Spring 1966):68–88.

Flake, Chad J., ed. *A Mormon Bibliography: 1830-1930*. Salt Lake City: University of Utah Press, 1978.

Flake, Chad J. and Larry W. Draper, comp. *A Mormon Bibliography 1830–1930: Ten Year Supplement*. Salt Lake City: University of Utah Press, 1989.

Godfrey, Kenneth W. "A New Prophet and a New Scripture: The Coming Forth of the Book of Mormon." *Ensign* 18 (January 1988):6–13.

Hartley, William G. "Upon You My Fellow Servants." In *The Prophet Joseph: Essays on the Life and Mission of Joseph Smith,* 49–72. Edited by Larry C. Porter and Susan Easton Black. Salt Lake City: Deseret Book, 1988.

Hill, Marvin. "Brodie Revisited: A Reappraisal." *Dialogue* 7 (Winter 1972):72–85.

Hicks, Michael. *Mormonism and Music: A History*. Urbana: University of Illinois Press, 1989.

_____. "Poetic Borrowing in Early Mormonism." *Dialogue* 18 (Spring 1985):132–44.

Hill, Marvin. "The First Vision Controversy: A Critique and Reconciliation." *Dialogue* 15 (Summer 1982):31–46.

_____. "Joseph Smith and the 1826 Trail: New Evidence and New Difficulties." *BYU Studies* 12 (Winter 1972):223–33.

_____. "Money Digging Folklore and the Beginnings of Mormonism: An Interpretive Suggestion." *BYU Studies* 24 (Fall 1984):473–88.

Jessee, Dean C. "Joseph Smith and the Beginning of Mormon Record Keeping." In *The Prophet Joseph Smith: Essays on the Life and Mission of Joseph Smith*, 138–60. Edited by Larry C. Porter and Susan Easton Black. Salt Lake City: Deseret Book Company, 1988.

_____. "The Original Book of Mormon Manuscript." *BYU Studies* 10 (Spring 1970):259–78.

_____. "The Reliability of Joseph Smith's History." *Journal of Mormon History* 3 (1976):34–39.

Kimball, Stanley B. "The Anthon Transcript: People, Primary Sources and Problems." *BYU Studies* 10 (Spring 1970):325–64.

Kirkham, Francis W. *A New Witness for Christ in America: The Book of Mormon*. 2 vols. Salt Lake City: Utah Printing Company, 1967, 1959.

Lancaster, James E. "The Method of Translation of the Book of Mormon." *John Whitmer Historical Association Journal*. 3 (1983):51–61.

Launius, Rodger D. "A Survey of Priesthood Ordination: 1830–1844." *Restoration Trail Forum* 9 (May 1983):3–4, 6.

Matthews, Robert J. "How We Got the Book of Moses." *Ensign* 16 (January 1986):43–49.

Murdoch, Norman H. "Joseph Smith, the Book of Mormon, and Mormonism: A Review Essay." *New York History* 67 (1986):224–30.

Paul, Robert. "Joseph Smith and the Manchester (New York) Library." *BYU Studies* 22 (Summer 1982):333–356.

Porter, Larry C. "The Colesville Branch and the Coming Forth of the Book of Mormon." *BYU Studies* 10 (Spring 1970):365–86.

_____. "Dating the Melchizedek Priesthood." *Ensign* 9 (June 1979):5–10.

_____. "The Field Is White Already to Harvest: Earliest Missionary Labors and the Book of Mormon." In *The Prophet Joseph: Essays on the Life and Mission of Joseph Smith*, 73–89. Edited by Larry C. Porter and Susan Easton Black. Salt Lake City: Deseret Book, 1988.

_____. "Was the Church Legally Incorporated at the Time It Was Organized in the State of New York?" *Ensign* 8 (October 1978):8–11.

Quinn, Michael. *Early Mormonism and the Magic World View* Salt Lake City: Signature Books, 1987.

Searle, Howard C. "Authorship of the History of Joseph Smith: A Review Essay," *BYU Studies* 21 (Winter 1981):101–22.

Smith, Gregory. "America at 1830." *Saints Herald* 123 (September 1986):17–19.

Underwood, Grant. "Early Mormon Perceptions of Contemporary America, 1830-1846." *BYU Studies* 26 (Summer 1986):49–61.

Van Wagoner, Richard, and Steven Walker. "Joseph Smith: 'The Gift of Seeing.' " *Dialogue* 15 (Summer 1982):49–68.

Vogel, Dan. *Religious Seekers and the Advent of Mormonism*. Midvale: Signature Books, 1988.

Walker, Ronald W. "The Persistent Idea of American Treasure Hunting." *BYU Studies* 24 (Fall 1984):429–59.

Walters, Wesley P., and Richard L. Bushman. "Roundtable: The Question of the Palmyra Revivals." *Dialogue* 4 (Spring 1969):301–20.

Wheelock, Seymour E. "The Prophet, the Physicians, and the Medical School." *Dartmouth Medical School Alumni Magazine*. (Spring 1984):25–27.

Whitaker, David. "Almanacs in the New England Heritage of Mormonism." *BYU Studies* 29 (Fall 1989):89–113.

Wirthlin, LeRoy S. "Joseph Smith's Boyhood Operation: An 1813 Surgical Success." *BYU Studies* 21 (Spring, 1981):131–54.

WOMEN'S STUDIES

Arrington, Leonard J. "The Legacy of Early Latter-day Saint Women." *John Whitmer Historical Association Journal* 10 (1990):3–17.

____. "Persons for All Seasons: Women in Mormon History." *BYU Studies* 20 (Fall 1979):39–58.

Arrington, Leonard J., and Susan Arrington Madsen. *Sunbonnet Sisters: True Stories of Mormon Women and Frontier Life*. Salt Lake City: Bookcraft, 1984.

Beecher, Maureen Ursenbach. "The 'Leading Sisters': A Female Hierarchy in Nineteenth Century Mormon Society." *Journal of Mormon History*. 9 (1982):25–39.

____, and Lavina Fielding Anderson, eds. *Sisters in Spirit: Mormon Women in Historical and Cultural Perspective*. Urbana: University of Illinois Press, 1987.

Brunson, L. Madelon. *Bonds of Sisterhood: A History of the RLDS Women's Organization, 1831-1983*. Independence: Herald House, 1985.

Goodyear, Imogene. " 'The Legacy of Early Latter-day Saint Women': A Feminist Critique." *John Whitmer Historical Association Journal* 10 (1990):21–23.

Madsen, Carol Cornwall, and David J. Whittaker. "History's Sequel: A Source Essay on Women in Mormon History." *Journal of Mormon History* 6 (1979):123–45.

Morain, Tom. " 'The Legacy of Early Latter-day Saint Women': A Review." *John Whitmer Historical Association Journal* 10 (1990):18–20.

Scott, Anne Firor. "Mormon Women, Other Women: Paradoxes and Challenges." *Journal of Mormon History* 13 (1986–87):3–20.

Scott, Lyn, and Maureen Ursenbach Beecher. "Mormon Women: A Bibliography in Process, 1977–1985." *Journal of Mormon History* 12 (1985):113–27.

Tullidge, Edward W. *The Women of Mormondom.* New York: Tullidge and Crandell, 1877.

INDEX

Anderson, George Edward, 3–6, 8–9, 12–16, 158–159
Andrews, William, 180
Avon, CT, 166–177; cemetery, 170–71

Book of Mormon, 10–11, 85–93, 101, 108, 115–17, 120–21, 126, 142–43, 155–56, 158–59
Boston, MA, 32–37
Boylston Hall (Boston, MA), 35–36
Buffalo, NY, 101–104
"Burned-over District", 7, 85

Carter, Jared, 40
Church of Jesus Christ of Latter-day Saints (Mormon or LDS), founding of and first organization, 12–19, 55, 90–93
Cole, Abner, 88
Colesville, NY, 146–48
Cowdery, Oliver, 11, 66–67, 91, 114, 155–56, 159–60, 192–93
Cowdery, William, home site, 66–67
Columbia College (New York), 85–87
Connecticut, 165–77

Dartmouth College, 77–80
Doctrine and Covenants, 93

Erie Canal, 92, 95, 102, 126–128

Fayette, NY, 6–7, 12, 140–44
Fishers, NY, 129–30

Fox Islands, ME, 185–89

Gilbert, John H., Jr., 87–88, 124–25
Grandin, E. B. 87–90; bookstore, 89–90, 120–21

Hale, Emma, (Smith), 144, 145–46, 150, 152, 153–55, 157, 161
Hale, Isaac, 66, 149–50, 153–55; home site (Wells, VT), 68–69; home site (Harmony, PA), 156–57; tombstone, 161
Hale, Jonathan H., 185–89
Hanover, NH, 77–81
Harmony, PA, 152–63
Harris, Martin, 11, 85–87, 90, 96, 124; farm, 10, 125–26
Hill Cumorah, 10, 85, 115–18
Hyde, Orson, 72, 181–85, 190–91

Illinois, 16–19
Iowa, 18

James, Jane, 166
Johnson, Lyman E., 40–41, 72–73

Kimball, Heber C., 70, 130–31, 135–36, 138, 139; home, 136
Kimball, Solomon, home, 139–40
Kirtland, OH, 12–14, 95–96, 194–95
Knight, Joseph, 147–48, 163

Lebanon, NH, 74–77

Lewis, Nathaniel, home site, 68–69
Lovely Schoolhouse (Avon, CT), 172–73

Mack, Solomon, 50–51, 73, 165; family, 71–72; farm, 4–5, 53–54; mills site, 72
Maine, 179–89
Manchester, NY, 104–118; district school site, 113, 114
Massachusetts, 21–37
McKune Cemetery (Harmony, PA), 161–62
Mendon, NY, 130–40
Missouri, 12–16; temple site at Far West, 15
Moor's Charity School (Hanover, NH), 75, 78, 80
Murdock farm, Squire, 61–62

Nauvoo, IL, 16–18
New Hampshire, 71–81
New York, 83–148
New York City, 86, 96–97
Niagara Falls, 99–100
Norwich, VT, 61–62

Old Spanish Mine site (near Harmony, PA), 162–63

Palmyra, NY, 11, 89–90, 106, 118–28; cemetery, 124
Pennsylvania, 149–63
Philadelphia, PA, 150–52
Pine Grove Cemetery (Topsfield, MA), 26–27
Potter's Slough (near Montrose, IA), 18
Pratt, Orson, 40, 72–73
Pratt, Parley P., 32, 99, 101
Priesthood Restoration Monument (Harmony, PA), 159–60

Quaker Meeting Hall (Farmington, NY), 115

Randolph, VT, 49–50
Reorganized Church of Jesus Christ of Latter Day Saints (RLDS), 14, 19
Rhode Island, 190–93
Rigdon, Sidney, 29–32
Royalton, VT, 58–60

Sacred Grove (Manchester, NY), 7–9, 110–13
Salem, MA, 28–32
Seneca Lake (Fayette, NY), 144
Sessions, Patty B., 180
Sharon, VT, 5–6, 50–58
Sheldon, VT, 69–70
Smith, Alvin (brother of Joseph Smith, Jr.), 122–24
Smith, Alvin (infant son of Joseph Smith, Jr.), 161–62
Smith, Asael, 24, 26, 40, 44–45, 47, 71, 93; house, 94
Smith, George Albert, 3
Smith, Hyrum, 16, 29, 156
Smith, John, house, 94
Smith, Joseph, Sr., 23–24, 49–50; and Lucy Mack Smith, 44, 46, 48; and family, 45, 51–53, 59, 61–63, 74–75, 84–85, 90; farm site (Tunbridge, VT), 48–49; home (Manchester), 107–09; home site (Lebanon, NH), 75–77; home site (Sharon, VT), 55; log cabin site (Palmyra), 105–06
Smith, Joseph, Jr., 7, 10–12, 16, 55–58, 75–77, 85–91, 93, 96–99, 111–13, 150–52, 153; and Emma Hale Smith, 146, 153–55, 157–58; family, 155; home site (Harmony, PA), 158–59; Memorial and Monument, 4, 6, 55–58
Smith, Lucy Mack, 71, 80–81, 103–04, 114–15, 128
Smith, Dr. Nathan, 77, 78–81; house, 81
Smith, Samuel, Jr., 24–25, 26–27
Smith, Samuel H., 72–73, 91–92, 181–84, 190–91
Snow, Erastus, 40
South Bainbridge (Afton), NY, 144–46
Spenser, Catherine, 22
Spenser, Orson, 22
Stowell, Josiah, 162–63
Susquehanna River (PA), 11, 159–60
Swift, John, Memorial Cemetery (Palmyra), 122–24

Tarbell, Squire, home site, 145–46
Thompson, Lot, home, 176
Tomlinson Corner Cemetery (Mendon, NY), 138–39

Tomlinson Inn (Mendon, NY), 136–38
Topsfield, MA, 5, 23–2
Tunbridge, VT, 41–48; Universalist
  meeting house, 47–48; village store, 46

Vermont, 39–70

Wells, VT, 65–69
Wheeler Mill (Avon, CT), 171–72
Whitingham, VT, 63–65
Whitmer, David, 142, 156
Whitmer, Peter, Sr., home, 6, 141–43;
  reconstructed cabin, 143
Whitney, Newel K., 96
Woodruff family mill site, 174

Woodruff, Ozem, home site, 175–76
Woodruff, Phoebe, 189
Woodruff, Wilford, 167–77, 185–89

York, ME, 181–85
Young, Brigham, 17–18, 31, 63–65,
  131–35, 193; home site, 133–34
Young, John and Abigail, 63–65; home,
  132
Young, Joseph, 31, 63, 193
Young, Miriam Works, 132–33, 135,
  139
Young, Phineas Howe, home, 129–30
Young, Zina Diantha Huntington,
  100–101

T. Jeffery Cottle practices law in Orem, Utah. Before receiving his law degree from Lewis and Clark Law School in Portland, Oregon, he studied anthropology and public administration at Brigham Young University in Provo, Utah. Jeff's current research interests deal with early LDS Church history, historic photography, and various legal topics. Jeff has spoken in various settings in his legal profession and presented papers at professional history association meetings and symposiums. He lives in Provo with his wife, Michaela Voss Cottle.

Richard Neitzel Holzapfel teaches for the LDS Church Educational System in Irvine, California. Richard's academic degrees include a Bachelor of Arts in political science and a Master of Arts in history. He has completed graduate studies at California State University, Fullerton and at the University of California, Irvine. Richard's research interests include nineteenth-century American history and ancient history. He has published articles and presented papers in both fields of study. He is a contributor in the forthcoming multi-volume *Encyclopedia of Mormonism,* to be published by the Macmillan Company. He lives in Irvine, California, with his wife, Jeni Broberg Holzapfel, and their five children.

Jeff and Richard have collaborated on several articles, and the award-winning book entitled *Old Mormon Nauvoo 1839–1846: Historic Photographs and Guide* (Provo: Grandin Book Company, 1990).